Between a Rock and a Hard Place

Eadar Creag agus Aite Cruaidh
The Scottish Brown Family

Nancy Haight Penrose

Edited by Daphne Ffoulks-Jones and David Holmes.
Copyedited by Kerry Davie.
Original map design by Jitan Dahal.
Cover design by Dwayne Dobson.
Interior design by Ashley Russell Designs.

Published by NextGen Story: Custom Publishing.
www.nextgenstory.com

The mark of a Scot of all classes is that he remembers and cherishes the memory of his forebears, good or bad; and there burns alive in him a sense of identity with the dead even to the twentieth generation.

—Robert Louis Stevenson

In Memory of

Douglas Launce James Brown

1949–2023

Walking. I am listening to a deeper way. Suddenly all my ancestors are behind me. Be still, they say. Watch and listen. You are the result of the love of thousands.

—Linda Hogan

Contents

Part V: *Inherited Journeys: The Next Generation of Canadians*
The Family of Alexander "Sandy" Brown and Isabella Wood

Part VI: *Settling into Community*
The Family of John Duncan "Dunc" Brown and Blanche Cooper

Part VII: *Thank You for Dreaming*

Part VIII: *Reflections on Family*

Remember the Men from Whom You are Sprung
(Cuimnich Air Daoine O'n D'Thaing Thu)

—Quintus Horatiusf (Horace)

Introduction

The time that I've spent researching the history of my maternal Brown family over the last forty years has been an interesting, challenging, but always rewarding journey. You see, my mother's maternal ancestors were Browns from England, and her paternal ancestors were also Browns, but from Scotland.

In time, as if destiny had pulled them all together, these Browns, both English and Scottish, settled in the same small community on St. Joseph Island in Ontario, Canada. There were even some marriages between the two families to solidify that bond even further.

To add one more twist to the cord that binds these families together, the ancestors of my own Scottish Brown family inter-married with other Browns from the same area in Scotland. Kismet, I suppose, as though fate had intended right from the beginning that the various branches of this family tree would all spring from the same solid and deeply planted roots.

I clearly remember the day when my mother suggested that we visit my great aunt, Sarah Isabella Brown Rains, who she thought might be able to help me get started with my family history. (This was in the early days of my research before computers and the internet.) When we arrived at her home, Aunt Sarah was in the middle of making hot cross buns for

Easter, while also busily stripping wallpaper. As we had come unannounced, Aunt Sarah was embarrassed that her house was such a "mess", but she welcomed us with tea and cookies.

She seemed befuddled at first by my request. Why on earth would I want to know about my ancestors? That seemed to be how she felt. Perhaps it was a common feeling of her generation—that the past had not always been easy; we needed to look forward to good days, not backward to when times were tough.

However, she relented and provided me with a handwritten list of family members and descendants. Those names started me on my long and very personal journey—a deep dive into the history of my own family. I focused my efforts on the Scottish Browns on my mother's side who had come to Canada from Scotland.

When our family is asked to describe their Brown roots, their simple answer is that they were farmers from Scotland. However, the truth is a lot more complicated. They were much more than farmers. Their story runs deep and is one of ongoing resilience and perseverance. They took advantage of opportunities as they arose. It began on Scotland's rugged western coast on the islands of the Inner Hebrides.

During the Industrial Revolution, the Browns, like many other families, sought to find their place in the world by moving to the thriving, bustling city of Glasgow and also to the farms and green pastures of Avondale Parish in Lanarkshire, Scotland.

The reality of it, however, was that their story was a lot harder and bleaker than anyone today could imagine—particularly for the women of the family. They faced unimaginable challenges and endured deep despair. The journey and personal struggles of those who had the vision and courage to leave their homeland to find a better life would eclipse the hardships faced by anyone today. While many in my maternal Brown family emigrated to Canada, a few made the journey to the United States, Australia, and New Zealand, where they established new lives and created new histories for themselves.

As we Browns delve deeper into the history of our ancestors and learn about their struggles, successes, and even some long-standing mysteries, we come to realize that our Brown roots are an integral part of our identity and a testament to the strength of the human spirit. Their struggles and triumphs are part of the Canadian story, a key component in the development of the Canada that we know today.

Imagine you have been living with hardly a shilling to your name. Your wife and family have now placed their trust in you; they blindly follow you while supressing their fears. You leave the only home that you have ever known—saying goodbye to your parents, siblings, and friends, knowing that you will never see them again—then travelling to an unknown land and praying every day that you've made the right decision. This has to be better than what you've left behind.

This book chronicles the remarkable journey of the Brown family—a saga woven tightly with the threads of survival, resilience, and the enduring legacy of generations who planted their roots in Canada.

Our story begins with Alexander Brown, a shoemaker born in 1754, who was presented with the opportunity of a lifetime and moved his family clear across land and sea to Easdale Island in Scotland to better their circumstances. We will follow the lives of his sons and daughters and their descendants, who laboured and toiled in the slate quarries and who were servants, labourers, and farmers.

In all, we will explore five generations of Browns finishing with my mother, Emily "Betty" Brown (1934–2004). Each of the direct descendants will have an entry in this book, except for those ancestors I was unable to find much information about. A complete list of each generation can be found in Appendix A.

John Brown was the first to bring his family to Canada. The year was 1864. As newcomers, they encountered many hurdles and obstacles overcoming each one in turn. They needed to make a living to support their families, and the persistence, fortitude, and strength they possessed is evident in the legacy they left behind.

They instilled values, principles, and a strong work ethic into their children, so that they would grow up to be the best they could be. Although the Scots are by nature a practical, common-sense lot, they did dream—they dreamt of a better future, and they worked diligently to turn that dream into a reality. Their philosophy was that no matter how long it took, if they worked hard enough and were open to opportunities, their dreams would come true.

It took nearly twenty years from their arrival in their new home country before they had fulfilled their dream of building a stable life for their families. Their sheer determination and steady focus allowed them to acquire their own land, a feat that would have been impossible in their native Scotland. They maintained (and even enhanced) that same determination, focus, and work ethic that had been handed down to them from previous generations.

My Brown ancestors embodied strength, dignity, and courage. Each day they pursued their goals with unwavering purpose undaunted by the challenges that lay ahead. Such a life was not meant for the faint-hearted, the weak-willed, or the idle. It demanded grit and an unyielding commitment to a dream.

As their descendants, we Browns owe it to them to carry forward this legacy of hard work and perseverance, to honour their memory, and to inspire future generations with their steadfast example.

From the Isles' northern most realm
Came the Scot bred with the stoutest will the canniest wit
and the bravest heart
For reasons dire did Scots forsake kin and kith and set
across the face of the earth to fend for themselves and in
the process, they built nations, empires and new worlds.

—Author Unknown

Brown Family Crest.[1]

Part I
Our Scottish Roots

Ar Freumhan Albannach

What's in a Name?

The Brown surname is one of the most common in all English-speaking countries and the second most common surname in Canada and Scotland. Its origin is in reference to the colouring of hair, complexion, or clothing.

In Scottish Gaelic, the language that our Scottish Brown ancestors used in their daily lives, the name Brown is translated as Mac-a-Bhruithainn (pronounced mac-avroon), which is roughly pronounced "bro-an."

The Brown or Broun tartan colours are red, black, mid-blue, and green.

For many centuries, the Scots followed a relatively simple set of rules when naming their children. While these traditional naming patterns were not followed by all families, they were widespread enough that a basic understanding can be very helpful when hunting for ancestors and their roots. Being familiar with these patterns has helped me greatly in identifying potential new ancestors, and it has helped to reveal all sorts of clues.

For boys, the naming pattern was:

First son named after his paternal grandfather
Second son named after his maternal grandfather
Third son named after his father

For girls, it was common to see:

First daughter named after her maternal grandmother
Second daughter named after her paternal grandmother
Third daughter named after her mother

Another common naming tradition was to use the mother's maiden name as a middle name. Scots are also known for using nicknames. Their birth registration may show their official name, but the individual was likely referred to by their nickname all their life. These are some examples found in the Brown family:

Given Name	Nickname	Gaelic Equivalent
Donald	Donnie	Domhnall
Dugald	Dougie	Dughall
Janet	Jane or Jessie	Teasag
Sarah	Sally or Sadie	Morag
Amy	Emily	Aimil
Helen	Ellen or Ellie	Eilidh
Alexander	Sandy	Alasdair

My research of over forty years has resulted in the discovery of twenty-two John Browns, eight Donald Browns, and seven Duncan Browns. The most common female names discovered were Sarah, Margaret, and Mary. With Brown being one of the most common surnames and with the repetition of first names, to say that it has been challenging to differentiate the Browns is an understatement. It's proven to be the linguistic equivalent of looking for that needle in a haystack!

While the tradition of how first names were given is generally no longer adhered to among contemporary members of the family, we can look back and view it as evidence of how each Brown saw himself as part of the overall Brown family story—an ongoing tale that continues to this day.

Scotland Our Ancestral Home

The Scottish Wifey.[2]

D NA results and Scotland's history reveal that it's very likely that some of the first Brown ancestors originated thousands of years ago in Scandinavia, as did many other Scots.

The first recorded history of my maternal Brown ancestors is the story of Alexander Brown in the mid-1700s in Scotland. In this period of history, Scotland was going through tumultuous change, both politically and economically. The country was ruled by George III of England, and it was legally a portion of Great Britain; as a result, the English influence was felt everywhere, including in the language spoken.

While the Gaelic language was still commonly spoken, its usage was in definite decline especially in the larger population centers. That wasn't the case in the more rural sections of the country, especially in the Highlands and among the island communities, including those of the Inner Hebrides where the Browns lived.

Alexander (1754–?) and his family lived in Scotland on the Island of Easdale, situated in the Firth of Lorn. Easdale is less than one hundred meters off the Isle of Seil. Easdale, Seil, Luing, and Belnahua are the principal Slate Islands of the Inner Hebrides in the historic county of Argyll, Scotland. The Inner Hebrides (Na h-Eileanan a-Staigh, "The Inner Isles") is an archipelago of islands located off the west coast of mainland Scotland. They are made up of thirty-five inhabited islands. As well, there are forty-six uninhabited islands each with an overall area greater than seventy-four acres. To the northwest of these islands are another archipelago, the Outer Hebrides. These inner and outer island chains collectively form the Hebrides.

Easdale Island.[3]

Slate Islands.[4]

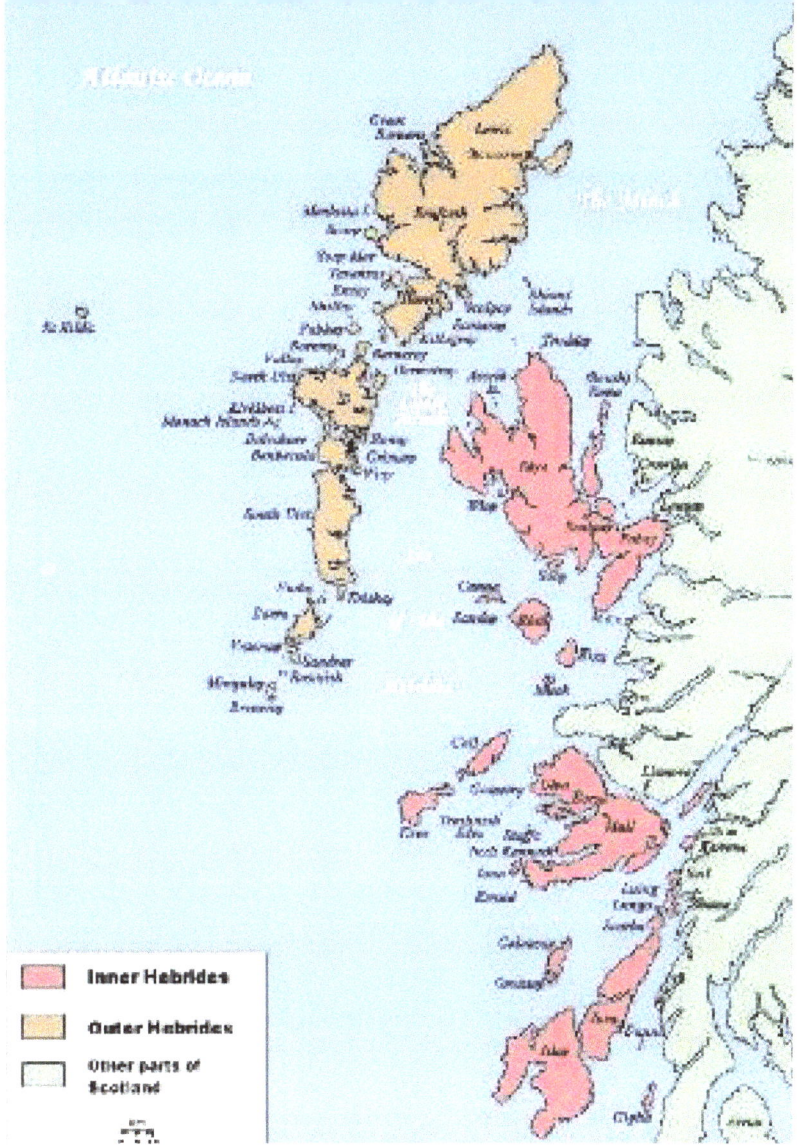

The Hebrides.[5]

From the historical records we can gain a clear insight into specific aspects of the daily lives of those living on Easdale Island, in particular Alexander Brown (1754–?), his wife Christian McDonald (1756–?), and their children. This includes what their meals consisted of and the special holidays that they celebrated.

Being on an island, the Browns' diet regularly included a variety of shellfish, oysters, mussels, lobster, prawns, and scallops. While today we often consider these "fruits de mer" to be delicacies, in those days, and on those islands, they proved to be a plentiful food source, often used as filling for soups and stews. Fish was routinely cured and smoked, herring was pickled in brine, and cod's head was a special treat. Salmon was so plentiful in those days that it was considered a poor man's meal, rather than the gourmet's delight it is today. Due to the size and nature of the island, there was no available space for grazing livestock, although some residents did own a cow or two as well as chickens. This would have provided some relief from a near constant diet of fish.

Fresh fruit and vegetables were a rarity (other than tatties (potatoes), cabbage, and neeps (turnips), while oats and barley were another staple part of the diet. During times when work was limited, the poorest families were allocated a boll (roughly 136 kg) of oats and barley by the parish council. This would be added to whatever the family could catch in the sea or gather from the land until more work became available.

The family of Alexander Brown had come to Easdale to pursue economic opportunities, so they were not among the poorest families there, though they had been among the poorest on the island of Luing where they had moved from.

The biggest celebration of the year for the community, and for Alexander and his family, was Hogmanay, or New Years. The Church of Scotland discouraged the celebration of Christmas, and the celebration was frowned upon for many years.

(It wasn't declared an official holiday in Scotland until 1958.)

In preparation for the new year, "redding the house" for Hogmanay began. This was much like a spring cleaning. It was believed to be bad luck to enter a new year with an untidy home. Redding the house involved a thorough cleaning and decluttering of the home, paying any outstanding debts, and clearing any old ashes from the fire. This was all to be completed before the celebration of the new year.

The festivities commenced with bonfires, and the community carried torches as they marched and sang Gaelic songs. Inside the community hall, the air was humming with excitement as the fiddlers tuned their instruments. Everyone would soon be dancing.

Couples like Alexander and Christian twirled in intricate patterns as the room reverberated with the rhythm of a traditional Scottish reel. In the corner, a table groaned under the weight of a massive wassail bowl, a traditional wooden bowl used during ceremonies and special occasions. It was brimming with spiced ale, apples, and cloves. The Browns and their neighbours would toast to health, prosperity, and kinship with a hearty cheer of "slàinte mhath!" (good health!).

As the clock struck midnight, the "first-footer" entered, a tall dark-haired man bearing gifts of salt, whisky, shortbread, coal, and a black bun (a fruitcake covered in pastry). Anything less to mark the date would result in bad luck. At end of the celebration, all would join hands and sing "Auld Lang Syne," a tribute to old friendships and memories. With voices raised in unison, all would shout "Lang may yer lum reek!", which means "May your chimney smoke long!", signifying a prosperous home.

Hogmanay Celebration.[6]

The Browns who lived in the Inner Hebrides spoke Scottish Gaelic and continued to use it when they arrived in Canada. The language is believed to have come from Ireland in the fourth and fifth centuries and was spoken mainly in the Highlands and on the islands of western Scotland. While its use was discouraged at school, the Brown children continued to speak Gaelic with their families at home.

At the time of Canadian Confederation in 1867, shortly after the Browns arrived in Canada, Gaelic was the third most spoken language in Canada, after English and French.

From the picture we get of what life was like for the original Scottish Browns, we can see that they lived close to the land and were community minded. The generations that came to Canada and grew their families here carried on these traditions, and they added their own unique ways of expressing these deeply rooted family values.

Why is it that my heart stirs
When I hear the bagpipes play
Why do I feel Scotland is my home
When I live so far away
Why do I feel a sense of pride
When I see the Saltire fly
Although it may seem strange to you
Perhaps I can tell you why
When you are born of Scottish blood
Something strange seems to take place
As if a seed is planted within you
Which makes you fiercely proud of your race
This Scottish patriotism never dies
And in your soul it always remains
Because Scotland is as much a part of you
As the blood flowing through your veins

—S. Mortazavi

Part II

Settling on Easdale Island
Tuineachadh air Eilean Easdale

The Family of Alexander Brown and Christian McDonald

Life in the Slate Quarries

Master Shoemaker and Apprentices.[7]

Although we cannot be certain where Alexander Brown was born in 1754, we do know that by the time he was twelve or thirteen years old he was working as an apprentice shoemaker, or "souter," as they were called in Scotland. Under the guidance of a master shoemaker, it would have taken him seven years to become a master himself. In those days, making boots and shoes was an arduous and time-consuming process; it would take between fourteen to eighteen hours to craft a single pair of boots.

On February 8, 1780, in the Parish of Kilbrandon and Kilchattan on Luing, one of the Slate Islands in the Inner Hebrides, Alexander married Christian McDonald. Three years later, the couple welcomed their first child, a son they named Dugald. In 1784, when their second child, Janet, was born, it seems that the family was struggling financially. Janet's birth registration states that Alexander and Christian could not afford to pay the registration fee and were labeled as poor.

Isle of Luing.[8]

Alexander's circumstances were about to change, however, as shortly thereafter he was offered a position as a shoemaker with the Marble and Slate Company on Easdale Island. He packed up his tools and his family and made the ten-kilometer journey, including two water crossings, to Easdale Island. Seil,

Belnahua, Luing, and Easdale were the principal slate-producing islands of Argyll. Still, it was Easdale that was the centre of the British slate industry. Slate from there was exported and used for construction in many major cities far and wide, and can still be seen on rooftops in Melbourne, Dublin, and even Nova Scotia. Although Alexander may have been the first of the Brown family to take up residence on Easdale Island, at least four generations of the Browns would eventually live and work as slate quarriers and labourers there, including all of Alexander's sons. Alexander himself also worked as a slate quarrier there, in addition to being a shoemaker.

Cullipool Harbour, Isle of Luing.[9]

Easdale slate, a distinctive black carbonaceous pyritic slate, had been collected from the shores of Easdale and surface-quarried for centuries before its commercial development began in the early eighteenth century. In 1745, the Marble and Slate Company of Netherlorn, Scotland, took over the quarries' management. At that time, eight crews of four men on Easdale produced approximately one million slates annually. By 1771, the workforce had grown to thirteen crews.

The unique natural cleavage in the slate rock allowed it to be split using tools into large, flat sheets. Despite its toughness, these sheets could be divided into precise thicknesses ranging from 12 mm to 6 mm without fracturing. Skilled cutters capitalized on this property to craft slates of the desired dimensions, making them ideal for roofing. Alexander and his sons were integral members of teams comprising of five or six workers; two quarriers, two splitters (known as nappers), and two labourers responsible for supplying rock to the nappers, as well as handling the finished slates and clearing the spoil.

The men who dressed the slate worked as close to the rock face as they could. They created rectangular pits in the ground, neatly reinforced with dry stone walling. To keep out the rain and the wind, corner posts supported a canvas or corrugated iron roof that protected them while they worked. The men often sat in the water that collected around them as they split and shaped the slates throughout their shift. The work was backbreaking; it was also dirty work, as slate creates a dust like coal.

As an employee of the Marble and Slate Company, Alexander rented one of the cottages on the island. In 1745, the earliest cottages on the island were built as accommodation for employees and their families by the Marquis of Breadalbane owner of the Marble and Slate Company. Initially, the cottages had central hearths and were thatched with reeds or heather. Windows were shuttered, not glazed.

Slate Quarrier.[10]

In the late eighteenth century, the company agreed to supply slate for roofing the cottages. Seconds or poorly shaped and small slates that could not be sold were used. It was during this time that coal was introduced to replace peat as fuel. Gable end chimney flues and stacks were also introduced then. There were about 115 cottages during the time period of the peak production of slate.

Cottages Easdale Island.[11]

There were two sizes of cottages, with the smallest consisting of one room used as a kitchen and living room, a bedroom, and a small storage area. The largest consisted of one main room, a bedroom separate from the main room, and a narrow room used as a pantry. The main room was approximately 4.5 meters by 5 meters, the pantry 3.5 meters by 1 meter, and the small bedroom 7 meters by 2 meters. There was also a front entrance hall about 1 meter square. Alexander and his family would have lived in this larger cottage layout.

Map of Cottages Easdale Island 1886.[12]

The interior consisted of lime-washed slate walls, slate flag-stone floors, and exposed ceiling joists. The attic was used as a bedroom by the children or young men and was an open area under the rafters.

Most of the cottages had a small garden where food was grown and several homes had a detached garden where the likes of "tatties" (potatoes), cabbage, and turnips, called "neeps," were grown. Seaweed was routinely used as fertilizer. As this was an island dominated by slate, there was little if any topsoil to grow a garden. So, this little Scottish island used Irish soil to grow its food. Ships from Belfast and Dublin used soil as ballast. When they arrived at Easdale to pick up their slate, they left the soil behind for the Easdale gardens—a win-win for both parties.

With about 160 cm of rain annually on Easdale, there was plenty of rainwater for Alexander and his family to collect for washing, cleaning, and other uses. As they still say in Scotland on a rainy day, "It's bucketin doon." Fresh drinking water was brought in barrels to Easdale by boat until, in later years, a lead pipeline was installed under the ocean from a reservoir on the nearby Isle of Seil.

Records seem to indicate that Alexander and Christian did leave Easdale in the early 1790s, as some of their children were born possibly on Tiree, Luing, or perhaps Coll Island all of which are in the Inner Hebrides archipelago. All together, they had seven children, though very little is known about their daughters Janet, born in 1784, and Catherine, born in 1791, and their son John, born in 1792.

As work became more available, their children did return to Easdale Island and they stayed there for the remainder of their lives, working as labourers and slate quarriers. Women and children were not exempt from work in the quarries either.

They carried the made slates in baskets on their backs or in wheelbarrows to the harbour for stacking. Some mechanization in 1790 meant that children were no longer required to do this heavy work. It was around this time that the Breadalbane Estate built a school for the children of Easdale Island.

Easdale Island Side School Easdale Island c1900.[13]

It is uncertain when Alexander or Christian died. What we do know, however, and will see throughout our story, is that the Browns never turned away from an opportunity. If uprooting their family to improve their situation was what it would take—as Alexander did with the move to Easdale Island—then pacaich agus rachamaid—pack up and let's go!

Dugald Brown (1783–1862)
Wages and the Company Store

A slate quarrier all his life, Dugald was the eldest son of Alexander Brown and Christian McDonald. He was born in 1783 on Luing Island, and he relocated to Easdale Island with his parents as a young boy. It is believed he married Mary McCallum in about 1805.

Life was hard and money scarce for the young couple. Men were not paid until the slate was sold, so in the meantime they ran up a debt at the company store. When they were finally paid, most of the money went to pay off their debt, leaving little for future expenses or savings. In 1796, after much negotiation, the company did pay the men for unsold slate. That policy didn't last long however, as the company once again reverted to the old system in 1799.

Government pensions were not introduced until 1909 in Scotland. Dugald was still working as a slate quarrier well into his seventies. If you didn't have savings to support yourself in your old age, you continued to work or were dependant on family to support you. Dugald died in 1862 at the age of seventy-nine, and his wife Mary died a few years later, in 1866, at the age of eighty-three. Dugald and Mary had five children.

For obvious reasons, there is no cemetery on Easdale Island. When an individual passed away, the remains were taken by boat to Seil, then carried about three kilometers to the Kilbrandon Parish Cemetery in Balvicar, a small village on the Island of Seil. Enroute, there were stone plinths (pillars) that the remains could be placed on in order for the cortège to rest and have a wee dram (small drink of whisky), something they probably were very grateful for.

The remains were placed on the plinths because it was believed that if they were put on unconsecrated ground, the souls of the deceased would be stolen by the devil. Some of the grave-stones of my Brown ancestors are slabs made from Easdale slate, cut and inscribed by the families themselves. Some are flat on the ground and not upright as we would traditionally see a grave marker today. Most, if not all are now hidden by overgrown grass and weeds.

Kilbrandon Old Churchyard, Balvicar, Isle of Seil.[14]

Kilbrandon Old Churchyard, Balvicar, Isle of Seil.[15] Alexander Brown.
Died September 2, 1878. Great-grandson of Dugald Brown
and Mary McCallum and their family.

Duncan Brown (1789–1874)
Advances in Machinery

Pumping Machinery.[16]

The second son of Alexander Brown and Christian McDonald was Duncan Brown. He was born in 1789 and was the father of John Brown (1818–1901), who would eventually settle on St. Joseph Island in Canada. Duncan was born on Easdale Island and remained there his entire life, working as a slate quarrier. He married Janet McDonald on October 15, 1817. They lived in Cottage #24.

In 1800, pumping machinery was introduced, allowing Duncan and the other men to work below sea level. This helped increase production to about five million slates per year. Some of the quarries extended all the way to ninety meters (three hundred feet) below sea level. There were at the time more than five hundred people working at as many as seven quarries on this sixty-two-acre island. It remains a centre to this day that has no roads. The island was thriving, and the harbour was filled with ships taking slate all over the world. At the age of seventy, Duncan was still working in the slate quarry.

Sometime between 1851 and 1855, Duncan's wife Janet died. He remarried on October 28, 1858, taking widow Christina Sinclair as his wife. Christina had been married to Archibald Fletcher, another quarrier on Easdale Island. Duncan and Christina lived in Cottage #23 from 1858 until Duncan's death in 1874 at the age of 85.

The photographer named the following photo The Hellish Rabble as he had difficulty getting the quarrymen to settle long enough to take the photo. The only individual we've been able to identify thanks to Allan MacDougall is the man to the right of the gentleman in the suit in the front row. He is Alexander McDougall who married John Brown's (St. Joseph Island) niece, Margaret Brown. Alexander and Margaret lived in Cottage #23 after Duncan and Christina died.

Slate Quarriers, Easdale Island.[17]

Donald Brown (1791–1865)
Making Time For Fun

Donald Brown was the third son of Alexander Brown and Christian McDonald. He was born in 1791, and he married Mary McCowan in 1814; he worked his entire life as a slate quarrier.

Donald and Mary had nine children. Though work took up much of their lives, the Browns of this generation did take some time for fun and entertainment. Sailing, fishing, picnics and, of course, ceilidh's (social gatherings for Scottish dancing) were all part of their recreational activities. Musical concerts and Highland games were also regularly held.

The sea was the primary link to the outside world for Donald and Mary's children. Quickly becoming skilled at boat handling, they learned the hard way how to navigate the channel between the islands of Easdale and Seil. Those wind-swept waters were often perilous, so they learned to read and to respect the winds and waves, and to reap whatever rewards washed ashore, especially those things that were either useful or edible. It was not a lifestyle that was given to waste, living as they did so close to survival every day.

As money was always in short supply, Donald continued to work as a slate quarrier until he was seventy. He died on May 15, 1865 at the age of seventy-four. His wife Mary lived until she was eighty-three, dying on November 12, 1878.

A stormy day (blawin' a hoolie) on the waters of Easdale Island.[18]

A paddle in the harbour of Easdale Island.[19]

Hugh Brown (1795–1869)
Shifting Between Occupations

Hugh, the youngest child of Alexander Brown and Christian McDonald, was born in 1792; he led a life marked by hard work and dedication. In 1841 his wife Ann McDonald died; he continued to live on Easdale and to work as a labourer. He also cared for his children: John (age fifteen), Christian (age fourteen), and Gilbert (age ten). His commitment to providing for his family was evident.

By 1851, Hugh's occupation had shifted to slate quarrying. This transition reflected the changing economic landscape of Easdale Island, as the slate industry underwent modernization and expansion. At this time, he was living with his daughter Mary and sons Dugald and John and he was still noted as a widower.

When Hugh reached the age of sixty-five, he was residing with two of his adult children and was listed as a former domestic servant. His resilience in raising his family after the passing of his wife and his adaptability to shift occupations were evident throughout his life.

Just before Hugh's passing in 1869 at the age of seventy-four, the Marble and Slate Company dissolved, and various other companies took over the quarries. Despite these changes, slate production remained a vital industry on the island, and the population of Easdale Island stood at approximately 450 people at the time.

Hugh's legacy endured through his six children—a testament to his unfailing dedication to his family, and to the enduring spirit of the people of Easdale Island.

Island of Seil with Easdale Island in the distance.[20]

A family known for its inventive and industrious nature; the Browns of the day quickly adapted to the emerging technologies of the time—after all, this was the dawn of the Industrial Revolution.

As mechanization became available, they embraced it, learning new skills and finding innovative ways to introduce the means to be even more productive. No strangers to hard work, they took on the challenges with even greater vigor, as they had families to support and a community to help grow. It's almost as if toil brought out the best in them.

The Browns were also very community-focussed, and they did their part to help foster a true sense of community spirit. Living isolated as they did, the Browns relied on each other and on their neighbours for support. This involved both work and play, which helped keep their spirits up while creating a sense of belonging.

This generation of Brown men lived well beyond the expected lifespan of men of this period, which is especially remarkable given the harsh working conditions, exposure to dust, and the hazardous conditions that they dealt with daily.

For example, the sons of Alexander and Christian lived an average of seventy-eight years, well beyond the forty-to-forty-five-year average of this period. Perhaps it was genetics, physical activity, or strong family support that contributed to a longer life.

> Perhaps it was simply a love of life that prolonged them, coupled with a "never say die" attitude that served them well in their native Scotland—and later in the new world that they would embrace.

Easdale quarry men.[21]

Part III

Leaving Easdale Island for the Next Opportunity
A' fàgail Eilean Easdail an Ath Chothrom

The Family of Duncan Brown
and Janet McDonald

Duncan (1789–1874) and Janet's (1790–1855) Children Off to Glasgow and Avondale

Continuing to trace the lineage of my maternal Browns, we now follow the family of Duncan Brown and Janet McDonald. All but one of their children left Easdale Island, seeking better lives for themselves in Glasgow and in the farming communities of Avondale. Perhaps they saw the writing on the wall. Competition for jobs on Easdale and the harsh conditions made them reconsider their future. Management of the quarries was inconsistent and even after years, how the workers were paid was still a bitter and contentious issue. The companies had agreed to pay the workers eight times per year; in some years by November, they had only received five payments. The workers often threatened job action and there were even threats of violence.

To add to the difficulties, in 1881 there was a horrendous storm, and at high tide, the entire island was flooded with water. Livestock were washed away; gardens were destroyed and about forty boats were lost. The quarries filled with water and the workers' tools and equipment in the pits were now under water—this left about 240 men and boys without work The slate industry on Easdale Island never fully recovered from this natural disaster.

Slate quarriers, Easdale Island.[22]

The last commercial slate taken from Easdale was shipped in 1911. By the time of the First World War in 1914, most of the young men still remaining on the island left to sign-up, leaving only old men and boys to do what little work there was in the quarries. The last slate was cut in the 1950s, and the once active quarries became abandoned, still pools, filled with water, and awash with memories.

Nevertheless, as we will soon discover, life on Easdale Island was relatively idyllic compared to the urban realities in Glasgow that some of Duncan and Janet's children would come to face. Despite their departure, the legacy of the Brown family and their contribution to the Island's slate industry was significant.

Just like for the thousands of others who moved to Glasgow during the Industrial Revolution, this would have been a culture shock for Duncan and Janet's children who relocated there. The city was a booming industrial hub, with shipbuilding, textile mills, flour mills, and various other manufacturing industries. From 1821 to 1901, the population of Glasgow grew from 147,000 to 762,000—an increase of over 400 percent!

Glasgow industries and pollution. Tradeston Gasworks.[23]

To house the growing workforce, tenement housing was built. They were notorious for overcrowding, no indoor plumbing, and no running water. They were also hotbeds for vermin and disease, with frequent outbreaks of cholera, typhus, and tuberculosis.

Eating, sleeping, and cooking took place all in the same room with families of six to a single room. Glasgow had developed a ticketing system for the tenements. Inspectors determined the number of people able to live within the square footage of each dwelling. That number was then stamped into porcelain or tin and tacked above the door.

The inspectors made their rounds in the middle of the night, and if they found a dwelling with more people than the number noted above the door, the family was evicted into the street. It is not certain if any of Duncan and Janet's children were evicted during their time in Glasgow, but the living conditions they faced there were less than optimal, to say the least.

Glasgow slums. (Photo by Thomas Annan 1829–1887).[24]

Glasgow tenements (Photo by Thomas Annan 1829–1887).[25]

John Brown (1818-1901)
The Start of a Farming Legacy

O f the Browns who would live on St. Joseph Island, Ontario, John Brown was the first direct ancestor to set foot on Canadian soil. Born about 1818 on Easdale Island in the Parish of Kilbrandon and Kilchattan, Argyll, Scotland, he was the eldest of Duncan Brown and Janet McDonald's children.

It is not clear exactly when John left Easdale Island, but in June of 1841, when he was twenty-three years of age, John and his younger brother Alexander, age thirteen, were working as farm labourers in Avondale, Lanarkshire, Scotland for a man named William Dykes. He owned Hazliebank Farm which was located just south of Glasgow. At the time, Avondale was the third largest parish in the county of Lanarkshire[26] and it includes the town of Strathaven (pronounced Stray-ven). Avondale is a farming area with emphasis on dairy and cattle breeding.

Although John and Alexander worked hard and their days were long, they may have been better off than their siblings who were living in the crowded, noisy, dirty, and disease-infested city of Glasgow.

John Brown's move to Lanarkshire would be the beginning of four generations (or 136 years) of farming for the Brown family.

As a farm labourer, John was responsible for ploughing fields, planting, harvesting, and ensuring that the horses were in tiptop shape. Maintenance of the harnesses and equipment would have been a priority.

Behind the Plough.[27]

Ploughing is an art and, as we will see in our story, John learned a great deal and passed this skill down to his sons John and Alexander (Sandy), and in turn to grandson John Duncan Brown, who later won many awards for his perfect furrows.

In 1842, John married Janet Granger and the couple moved to nearby Hamilton, about thirteen kilometers from Strathaven. Over time they would have eight children. In 1864, when John was already in his late forties, he made the bold move to take his family to Canada—forever changing the fates and the history of the Brown family, as they became a vital part of this promising new land.

Janet Brown (1821-1855)
Descendants in Australia

Duncan and Janet McDonald's eldest daughter, who was also named Janet, married Duncan Henderson in 1842. In 1851, she and her children, Duncan age eight, Donald six, and Catherina four were living with her parents, Duncan Brown and Janet McDonald, on Easdale Island in Cottage #24. Her husband was working away. Like her siblings, Janet and her husband eventually made their way to Glasgow, where her husband Duncan obtained a job in a brewery. Sadly, on June 5, 1855, at the age of thirty-four, Janet died due to a miscarriage, leaving her husband and their five children behind.

Life's cruelty was far from done with the Henderson family. A month later, their youngest daughter, Mary, died when she contracted measles. She was less than a year old. One week later, their daughter Janet died of scarlet fever at just five years old. A lack of medical care and medicines during those times resulted in the untimely death of both mother and daughters. Duncan had no choice but to continue working so that he could support his children—regardless of the grief he felt.

During these hard days, society viewed child labour much differently than they do today. For example, the Factory Act of 1833 stated that children under the age of nine could not work in the textile mills that helped drive the regional economy.

However, when Janet died, two of her boys, aged ten and twelve, could have legally been sent to work, and they probably were.

With the father and the two eldest boys on the job, that would have left the youngest sibling, age eight, to fend for themself. Children of the day had to learn to be resilient and responsible much earlier than is now common in our modern world.

Child labour in Glasgow factories-1910.[28]

The following year, in 1856, Duncan Henderson married his second cousin, Ann Henderson. By 1880, Duncan was a widower once again. In 1895, Duncan died of debility (weakness) and bronchitis in the Barnhill Poorhouse in Glasgow; a sad end, but not an uncommon one in those hard days.

Children caring for children. Govan Street, Glasgow.[29]

The Janet and Duncan Henderson family was the first I had come across with a connection to Australia. Their eldest son, Duncan, married in 1867. In 1870, he, his wife, and infant son left aboard the Flying Cloud (a clipper ship) for the nearly four-month long journey to Queensland, Australia.

The clipper ship Flying Cloud.[30]

The age of mass migration.[31]

EMIGRATION.

o Small Farmers, Mechanics & Laborers.

The precious years of your life are passing away, while you are waiting for a relief that
y never come. The REAL REMEDY for your accumulated distress is in EMIGRATION.
Embrace the present favorable opportunity of leaving a Land "where you live BY TAKING
E BREAD OUT OF EACH OTHER'S MOUTHS."

n South Australia, Western Australia,
And NEW ZEALAND,

ou can be rewarded for your Labor, and bring up your Families in comfort, "free from the
ping curse of Poverty,"—and many, by industry, in a few years become INDEPENDENT
NDHOLDERS.

FREE PASSAGES

e offered to Persons of good Character, and every arrangement made conducive to your
comfort while on the Voyage and after you Land.

o the Clergy and Gentry, the Rich and the Intelligent—

elling that Poverty and Idleness are the chief promoters of Crime, they should assist the Poor
their Neighbourhood in reaching these Countries. And all Englishmen are interested in the
sperity of Colonies which contribute so much to the Wealth and Grandeur of this Country.

Every Information may be obtained on application (personally or by letter) at the

MIGRANT DEPOT, GROVE STREET, DEPTFORD,
And 15, FISH STREET HILL, LONDON.

Nathan, Printer, Callum-st. Fenchurch-st. London.

For some of the same reasons that many in Scotland left for Canada or the United States, some chose to settle in Australia, with assistance programs designed to fully or partially pay for their journey. There were not enough jobs available for everyone in Scotland, and the government worried that the population was growing faster than its resources could handle. It was a practical financial solution in their minds, to help ship some of these excess citizens to distant lands across the seas. The wealthier people in Scotland had to pay taxes to support the very poor, so if the poor migrated, they would cease to be a financial burden. Oh, the Scots, and their canny financial ways!

Donald Brown (1823-1887)
The One Who Stayed Behind

Duncan and Janet McDonald's son Donald became an apprentice quarrier in Easdale at age fifteen. This would be physically challenging work for anyone, let alone a young boy. It involved the heavy lifting, splitting, and trimming of slate. This harsh coastal environment and the long hours could take their toll on any man or boy. Donald was the only one of this generation to remain on Easdale Island. In 1847, he married Margaret McDonald. Donald lived in Cottage #72 and later Cottage #65 until his death. He died on October 21, 1887, at age 64. Donald and Margaret had a total of ten children.

Incidentally, Cottage #65, where Donald lived and died, has been refurbished and is currently rented out as a vacation cottage. It was recently listed for sale for the equivalent of C$383,000, which would be a huge sum even for the Marquis of Breadalbane, who built and owned the original cottages in 1745.

The story of Sarah, one of Donald and Margaret's children, gives insight into how challenging life was for the Browns of the 1800s and early 1900s, and how few societal supports were available to care for people in need.

About seventeen years after Donald's death, in 1904, Sarah found herself in dire circumstances. With seven children

Cottage #65 Easdale Island.[32]

ranging in age from fourteen to two years old, and with twins on the way, she was forced to apply for relief from the parish council. The reason for her hardship remains unclear, but it's possible that her husband was out of work or ill. Regardless of the circumstances, Sarah had to put aside her pride and explain to the council why she required assistance. However, simply receiving aid was no easy feat, as councils were notoriously stringent in their distribution of funds.

Nearly two decades later, Sarah found herself a widow, and she, along with six of her now ten grown children, emigrated to New Jersey, United States with $5,000. This would be the equivalent of more than $90,000 today, a sizable fortune at the time.

Sarah Brown Laird and her family. Back (left to right) Thomas, Duncan, William. Middle row (left to right) Donald, Margaret. Front row (left to right) Matilda, John, Sarah (mother), Sarah, Colin, Robert.

However, Sarah's stay in America was not permanent, and by 1930 she had returned to Scotland. Her life had come full circle, and in 1937 she passed away at age seventy-five on Easdale Island, the place where it all began. It is noted on her death registration that she had also suffered from senility.

Mary Brown (1825–1901)
Devoted Wife and Mother

Like almost all her siblings, Mary would make her way to Glasgow; she was about age sixteen. She was the fourth child of Duncan Brown and Janet McDonald. Mary was a servant who worked for Mr. and Mrs. Harper. Mr. Harper was a victualler, an uncommon term today, as it is someone who has been licensed and contracted to sell food and spirits to the Royal Navy. Mr. and Mrs. Harper had a busy household and business, employing six staff members.

Mary was among the fortunate few who received accommodation from her employer. Her living quarters were modest, and they were shared with fellow female servants; they were austere in their simplicity. However, a significant benefit was that the servants' meals were included as part of their wages. Despite the long hours and demanding work, the servants fared considerably better than the factory workers and the unemployed who resided in the streets and cramped tenement housing around the city—those people endured deplorable conditions and struggled simply to find food.

In 1848, a massive riot erupted in the very neighborhood where Mary lived. It spilt onto Graeme Street—the same street that the Harper's and their servants—including Mary—lived on. The impoverished and unemployed had reached a breaking point.

The government had made promises of distributing provisions, but these pledges remained unfulfilled.

On March 6, between four and five thousand of the starving and enraged took to the streets of central Glasgow, breaking into food and gun shops. Business ground to a halt, and shops were shuttered, yet the determined throngs pressed on through the streets, their rallying cry echoing: "bread or revolution!"

Authorities dispatched troops from Edinburgh in a bid to quell the unrest. Tensions reached a critical point when a young boy was apprehended, and the crowd surged against the troops in retaliation. Under the orders of the police superintendent, shots were fired, resulting in five casualties among the protesters. Mary and her housemates remained inside with the doors locked, occasionally peering through the windows to watch as the riot unfolded.

1848 riots in Glasgow.[32]

The military presence continued to patrol the streets for several days, an ominous reminder of the volatile times in which they lived.

Even with all the troubles in those years, Mary decided to stay in Glasgow and build her life there. In 1855, at the age of thirty, she married John Harroway, a canal boatman. Two years into their marriage, Mary and John embarked on a heartfelt journey by adopting a baby girl named Christina, affectionately known as Tinnie. She was born on May 11, 1857 to Christina Turner, an unmarried, hardworking factory labourer.

Canal Barge.[33]

The challenges of life in Glasgow during this era made single parenthood an immense burden, and nearly insurmountable. The societal stigma attached to having a child outside of wedlock only compounded the struggles.

Mary and John joyously welcomed their first biological child, a son named John, on August 19, 1859. Later, in 1861, they celebrated the birth of another son William. Unfortunately, William fell seriously ill in February 1868, at just six years of age. Mary dedicated herself to his care for two arduous weeks, but on March 3, they lost him to pneumonia.

Glasgow, like many other urban areas, suffered devastating illnesses which affected people from all walks of life, regardless of their social status. The air quality was heavily compromised by industrial pollution and coal fires. The most vulnerable members of society—the young and the elderly—bore the brunt of these harsh living conditions. Even into the 1890s, one out of every seven infants in Glasgow did not survive, succumbing primarily to common childhood illnesses like measles and diarrhea.

Tragedy and sorrow, stemming from the loss of children or parents when the children were at a young age, cast a shadow over most families—regardless of their financial standing.

During an era when great emphasis was placed on elaborate funerals and intricate mourning customs, the death of a loved one could impose a significant financial burden on a family. The shame associated with a pauper's burial weighed heavily on the hearts of those left behind, adding yet another layer of hardship onto an already challenging existence. Being of meager means, John and Mary would have experienced this additional emotional pain.

In the ensuing years, seeing their other children become established would have offered some consolation to the couple. Daughter Christina became a skilled milliner and in 1879 she married John Sanderson, a hatter (men's hat maker). To be successful in their trade, Christina and John would have apprenticed for about seven years under the guidance of a professional milliner/hatter. John expanded his business over the years, becoming a "ladies and gentlemen outfitter." Mary and John's son, John Jr., followed in his father's footsteps and became a canal boatman.

In 1889, a dark cloud descended upon the family when John Sr. received the devastating diagnosis of stomach cancer. Mary devoted herself to his care, doing everything in her power to ease his suffering and to ensure his comfort. This difficult journey came to an end in 1891 when John Sr. passed away on July 8.

The subsequent year brought a new chapter to their family story as John Jr. married Annie Stewart. Mary, in her later years, joined them in their home, becoming a cherished presence in their lives as they welcomed each of their children to their growing family.

Sadly, Mary's health deteriorated over time, and she struggled with cognitive decline. Her battle ended on September 2, 1901 when she passed away due to complications associated with senility, leaving behind a legacy of love and resilience.

Alexander Brown (1827-1868)
Small Decision, Big Consequences

A lexander, the son of Duncan Brown and Janet McDonald, left Easdale around 1840 with his brother John (1818–1901)—the brother who would make his way to Canada around 1864. The two brothers headed for Lanarkshire where they worked as farm labourers. Alexander subsequently left his job on the farm to work in a brewery in Glasgow, and in 1852 he married Catherine McQueen, also from Easdale Island.

Mixing the mash.[34]

On Saturday, November 16, 1868, Alexander would make a seemingly harmless decision that would have a profound and devastating impact not only on his own life—but also on the lives of everyone in his family.

While celebrating the end of a long work week, Alexander had one too many pints at the pub. On the way home he fell, breaking several ribs. A good Samaritan assisted him back to his home for rest and recovery. However, Alexander was unable to overcome his injuries, and two days later, he died. He left behind his wife and five children.

Tenement housing (slums), Duke Street
where Alexander and Catherine lived in 1861.[35]

FATAL ACCIDENT.—On Monday forenoon, a labourer named Alexander Brown, 42 years of age, residing at 136 Moore Street, expired in his own house from the effects of injuries he received on the evening of Saturday last, It appears that, while the unfortunate man was passing along Cumbernauld Road, somewhat affected with liquor, he stumbled and fell against a wall, whereby several of his ribs were fractured. He was assisted home, but never rallied, and expired on Monday.

Glasgow Herald, November 18, 1868.

How was Catherine going to manage? She had been a servant since the age of ten until her marriage at the age of twenty-three. She now needed another position such as this to support her children. Her options were to find employment and leave the children to their own devices, remarry, or receive support from her parish or other private sources. The last option would be the poorhouse, which was an absolute last resort due to the deplorable conditions there.

Catherine could neither read nor write but as became evident, she was quite capable and resourceful. She sent her three older boys, Duncan, John, and Peter, ages fourteen, twelve, and ten, out to work for a local butcher. John and Peter would continue in that line of work for many years. Catherine found work as a housekeeper and maintained this work for nearly seventeen years after her husband's death. Through her determination, she made sure that her family was provided for, and they avoided the poorhouse, which unfortunately was a common destination for women and their families in her situation at the time.

Glasgow butcher shop.[36]

Ten years after his father's death, eldest son Duncan left Scotland and emigrated to Queensland, Australia where he married and had six children.

Sometime between 1881 and 1885, Catherine returned to Easdale Island. It was there that her family began to be very concerned about her mental state—even more so after she attempted to drown herself. On April 29, 1885, she was examined by Dr. John Hunter, and he determined that she was of unsound mind. His notes indicated that she appeared to be incoherent, and she confessed that she had tried to drown herself.

Dr. Carmichael, a second physician, examined Catherine. He noted that she had stated that the devil had tempted her to drown herself, and she accused her daughter-in-law of maliciously spreading rumours about her having a loathsome disease. Catherine also believed her food was poisoned.

Her son Peter was summoned from Glasgow and was required to sign a document stating that his mother was in a state of mental derangement and that she should be admitted for treatment to the Argyll and Bute District Asylum. What a challenging and emotional experience this must have been for Peter!

Catherine was admitted and remained in the asylum for an astounding twenty-three years until her death in 1908 at the age of seventy-eight. Mental illness during these times was not well understood and treatment was often harsh, cruel, and sometimes dangerous. Often, there was social stigma and discrimination, and mental health challenges were viewed as a personal failing. There was very little hope of recovery or release—especially for the poor.

Argyll and Bute District Asylum.[37]

Seated: Peter Brown, son of Alexander Brown and Catherine McQueen, daughter Mary, and wife Mary. Standing: daughter Christina and son Alexander. Taken about 1909—one year after Peter's mother's death.

The same resilience that Catherine demonstrated following her husband's death—when she managed to hold her family together, a formidable accomplishment—appears to be what she drew on to live for more than two decades in the asylum. She was indeed an exceptionally strong woman.

Sarah Brown (1832–1896)
The Poorhouse

By 1851, Duncan Brown and Janet McDonald's daughter Sarah had also moved to Glasgow and was working as a servant/nurse for the Cree family. The nurse designation means that Sarah was likely a nanny; Mr. Cree was an insurance broker, and he and his wife Alice had two small children.

At the age of twenty-nine, Sarah married Donald McKay in Glasgow, on June 7, 1861. He was also from Easdale Island, and he held a variety of jobs, with the last being as a ferryman in the harbour in Glasgow.

Ardgowan Place, Glasgow, where Sarah and Donald lived in 1871. [38]

Glasgow ferryman.[39]

Donald died in 1872 at the age of forty-four, leaving Sarah with
five children ranging in age from eight to two years old,
including six-year-old twins, Jessie and Ann. Once again, we
find one of the Brown women a widow with small children to
care for. There were no social programs like welfare, daycare,
or assistance of any kind for women who found themselves
in Sarah's predicament.

What happened next was as devastating and heartbreaking as anything found in a Dickens novel. Months after her husband's death, Sarah was admitted to the Govan Poorhouse in Glasgow, where she was placed in an asylum. This institution (the poorhouse) included a 180-bed asylum and a 240-bed hospital. Patients in the asylum were referred to as pauper lunatics.

Children living in the tenement housing in Glasgow.[40]

There was no public health care, and admitting oneself to the poorhouse for medical treatment was often the only choice. Sarah was destitute with nowhere to turn and spent several months here before being discharged. This would, however, not be the last she would see of the asylum.

If the conditions in tenement housing were horrendous, the conditions in these asylums were even worse. A commission report prepared by one attending physician stated in part,

> The portion of the house in occupation was considerably overcrowded, and the patients were indifferently attended to. Three female patients of dirty habits occupied a room measuring about 12 feet long, 8 feet broad, and 10 feet high, equal to 960 cubic feet. They sleep in trough beds, on loose straw covered by a sheet; the straw is changed without sufficiently cleaning the bedstead, which, on removing the fresh straw, we found saturated with urine. Some of the sleeping-rooms were very close and offensive. They have one paid attendant and two pauper assistants.

Destitute mother and baby—tenement housing Glasgow.[41]

On July 12, 1873, just a few short months after she was discharged from the asylum, Sarah's neighbours contacted authorities over concern for her. A certificate of emergency was submitted by the sheriff for Sarah's admission to the Govan Lunatic Asylum, part of the Govan Poorhouse.

Comments from the attending physician stated,

> I have this day seen and personally examined Sarah Brown McKay at the Govan Parochial Lunatic Asylum and hereby report and certify with respect to her mental state that it is due to depression and melancholy.

Further comments stated, "Patient has a mild startled appearance, mutters occasionally to herself but refuses to answer questions." It was also noted that Sarah had been drinking, which would complicate her mental state.

Her neighbour, William Wallace, stated that Sarah had been confined to an asylum previously and that she was afraid of losing her children, the eldest being nine and the youngest age three. Another neighbour, Mrs. McDonald, said that she had tried to provide Sarah and her family with some food, but Sarah had refused to take it, believing that she couldn't afford it. Mrs. McDonald said Sarah shouted and screamed without cause, and that she had seen her eating filth.

Sarah was diagnosed with an "unsound mind." Her children were kept at the Govan Poorhouse during her stay in the asylum. In the early morning hours, on a cold spring morning in April 1874, her son Archibald, just five years old, died of bronchitis.

This poor little child died without his mother to embrace or comfort him during his final hours. His death registration labels him a pauper, a poignant reminder of the struggles and hardships endured by this family. As if his life held no meaning, Archibald was buried in a common unmarked pauper's grave. Sometime later, Sarah was released from the asylum.

As if her life hadn't been tragic enough, just a few years later, in 1879, Sarah's daughter Jessie died at age twelve of tuberculosis, a common cause of death during this period due in part to the deplorable living conditions. As Sarah could neither read nor write, her "X" (her mark) appears on the death registration, acknowledging that she had been present when Jessie passed away. Although her child was not labeled a pauper this time, it is unlikely that Sarah would have had the means to bury her, and Jessie would have been laid to rest in a common pauper's grave.

Within just seven years, Sarah had lost her father, her husband, and two of her children.

Sarah's surviving children demonstrated a strong sense of commitment and love for their mother by taking on the responsibility of caring for her over the years—at least for as long as they could—a testament to their devotion to family.

By 1881, Sarah was living with her children: John, sixteen, a message boy, Annie, fourteen, a domestic servant, and Donald, age ten, who was attending school. Sarah was working as a charwoman in Glasgow. Although three of them were working, they tittered on the edge of poverty for many years.

Tragically, in 1896, Sarah found herself once again in the Glasgow City Poorhouse, this time for the last time. She passed away there on November 24 at the age of sixty-four and was labeled a pauper, marking a somber ending to her life.

The imposing façade of the Glasgow City Poorhouse, taken in 1880.[42]

***

It is intriguing to contemplate whether individuals like Alexander Brown (1827–1868) ever envisioned that their legacy would be so meticulously examined by their descendants—a century and a half later. Imagine the astonishment he might feel knowing that we can now delve into historical newspapers which detail the unfortunate circumstances of his fall and subsequent death.

Consider the reflections of Sarah Brown McKay (1832–1896) and Catherine McQueen Brown (1829–1908), both of whom had been confined to asylums, and how surreal it would be for them to fathom that future generations would unravel the records of their challenging predicaments. If they had possessed a crystal ball granting them a glimpse into the future, what emotions would have been stirred within them as they observed the advancements in medical treatment, our quality of life, and in the well-being of their descendants?

How would they feel about the fact that the Brown family had over the years become landowners, successfully pursued multiple careers outside of farming, and become productive members of their communities? It's because of their perseverance, determination, and pursuit of opportunities that we are here now. Would they be proud, saddened, or concerned at what they see in the world today?

The story of the Brown family during the Industrial Revolution is undeniably a heart-wrenching account that highlights the multifaceted impact of this era. Amidst the newfound opportunities that it presented, the Browns encountered not only success, but also the harsh realities of poverty, illness, and untimely death.

It would be Duncan and Janet McDonald's son John (1818–1901) who would come to stand as a beacon of hope, bringing the

Browns to Canada with a powerful combination of hard work, unwavering determination, and a stroke of good fortune.

The next part of our story will serve as a poignant reminder of life's unpredictable nature and the paramount importance of seizing every opportunity that crosses our path.

Queen's Dock, Glasgow, 1878.[43]

Part IV

Farewell Bonny Scotland: To the Colonies
Soraidh Bonny Alba: Gu an Coloinidhean

The Family of John Brown and Janet Granger

Leaving Scotland, land of heather and song, with a
heavy heart, I bid thee so long. The hills and glens,
where memories reside, shall fade from view,
as I must now decide.
No more the bagpipes' mournful, haunting strain,
shall fill my soul with longing and with pain. The lochs,
like mirrors, sparkling in the sun, shall be a distant
dream when day is done.
The castles, ancient, crumbling in the mist, shall be but
shadows of the past I've kissed. The tartan plaid, a
symbol of my kin, shall be a memory, lost in the wind.
For I must go, to lands unknown and new, to seek a
future, bid the old adieu. But in my heart, Scotland,
you'll ever burn, a love eternal, for which I'll yearn.
Though I may never tread upon your soil, your spirit in
my soul shall never spoil. For Scotland, you are woven in
my soul, a part of me, forever, as I go.
And though I leave, I'll carry you with me, In every step,
in every memory. So, fare thee well, dear Scotland, never
fear, for in my heart, you'll always be right here.

—Author Unknown

John Brown (1818–1901) and Janet Granger (1821–?)
A Family on the Move

Duncan Brown and Janet McDonald's son John married Janet Granger in 1842. The Presbyterian minister Rev. William Proudfoot presided, and the ceremony was held at her parents' Priestgill farm, the place where she had grown up, located just south of Strathaven in South Lanarkshire, Scotland.

The Clyde Valley near Hamilton.[44]

Janet was the daughter of John Granger and Marion Meikle. At the time of their marriage, John was living in Hamilton, located about twenty kilometers from Priestgill. After their marriage, John and Janet settled in Hamilton which sits in the valley of the River Clyde, and which is known for its flat agricultural land. This is where they would spend the next five years building their life together. It's likely John continued as a farm labourer or a tenant farmer during this time.

Spinning wool.[45]

John worked in the fields, and Janet maintained their home. She washed and mended clothes, prepared meals, and worked their garden. Janet was not only a dedicated homemaker, but also a skilled weaver which added to the family's livelihood. John and Janet's days were filled with back-breaking work from sunrise to sunset, but we'd like to think that they were also filled with love and the satisfaction of working toward a goal together.

On January 1, 1843, they welcomed their first child, Marion Granger Brown. Her birth record was transcribed as Marion Grainger Browne. Two years later, in 1845, their second daughter Janet was born. After Janet's birth, an opportunity arose for the family to move to Crown House, Roman Road, Sandford, Strathaven. Census records refer to this dwelling as Five Shilling House.

The enumerator must have had a sense of humour, as five shillings equal a crown, and hence the reference to Five Shilling House instead of the official name of Crown House. The property would have been a familiar one for Janet, as her grandparents, the Meikle family, had owned it twice before.

John and family rented the house, and John farmed twelve acres of the property. It was while they were living at Crown House that they welcomed their third daughter Helen in 1848. In 1851, another daughter Mary was born into the Brown family.

In or about 1852, John and Janet relocated their family once more, this time to Burnhead, which is situated about eleven kilometers from Crown House in Sandford, Strathaven. This new location was at that time a small cluster of farms with

Crown House—taken in the 1850s.[46]

Crown House—present day.[47]

Burnhead Farm as it was in 2018.[48]

several families occupying and working various acreages; here John farmed about forty acres.

As fate would have it, tragedy darkened their door in May of 1853 when their young daughter Helen—just five years old—breathed her last. Infant and child mortality were commonplace during this time, but that did not lessen the grief and sorrow that John and Janet felt. As her life slipped away, a window was briefly opened to ease the passage of her soul, while mirrors and windows were covered in deference.

Helen's tiny body would have been prepared and dressed or wrapped in a shroud by her mother Janet and the other women of the village and then placed in a casket—if the Browns would have been able to afford one. The body would then have been laid out in the main room of their house. Flowers from the

Browns' garden and those of their neighbours would have likely adorned the room.

As a poignant tribute to Helen's brief life, the local church bell tolled five times, one for each year of her short life. John and Janet kept vigil until the time of the funeral, watching over little Helen and greeting mourners who came to pay their respects. John and his male neighbours carried the casket or shrouded body to the cemetery, with Janet, Helen's siblings, and villagers following behind. In accordance with the Scottish tradition of the time, only the men entered the cemetery while Janet and the other female mourners waited outside the gate.

Funeral procession.[49]

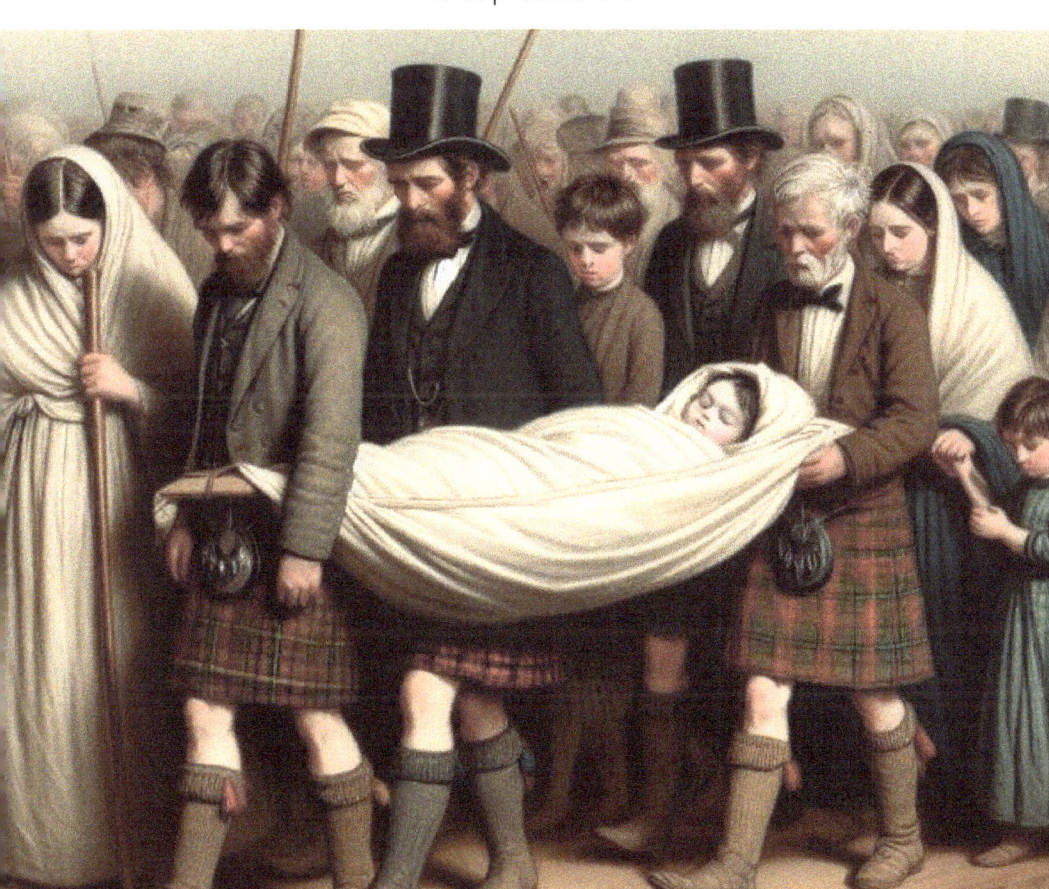

Living on the farm meant that John and Janet still had to milk cows, feed chickens, collect eggs, and attend to their surviving children. There was no bereavement counselling or leave for them to access. Although neighbours and friends would rally around them, they would have to carry on and endure their sorrow and mourning in silence, and alone.

This is a glimpse into the resilience of John, Janet, and their family. They faced immense hardships and tragedy with stoic determination, and they found solace in the routines of farm life while mourning the loss of their precious child, Helen.

When in 1854 a fifth daughter was born to John and Janet, in keeping with the tradition of the time, she was named Helen, after her deceased sister. However, while her birth registration officially recorded her name as Helen, she was commonly referred to as Ellen within her family and in various documents. Ellen is a Scottish nickname for the name Helen, and this reflects the practice of using these variants interchangeably.

Interestingly, when she eventually married several years later, Ellen took on the additional name of Annie. The reasons behind this choice remain somewhat mysterious, as name changes were not common during marriage ceremonies at the time. As a result, when she tied the knot, her name was recorded as Annie Ellen Brown, combining both Ellen and Annie into her official name.

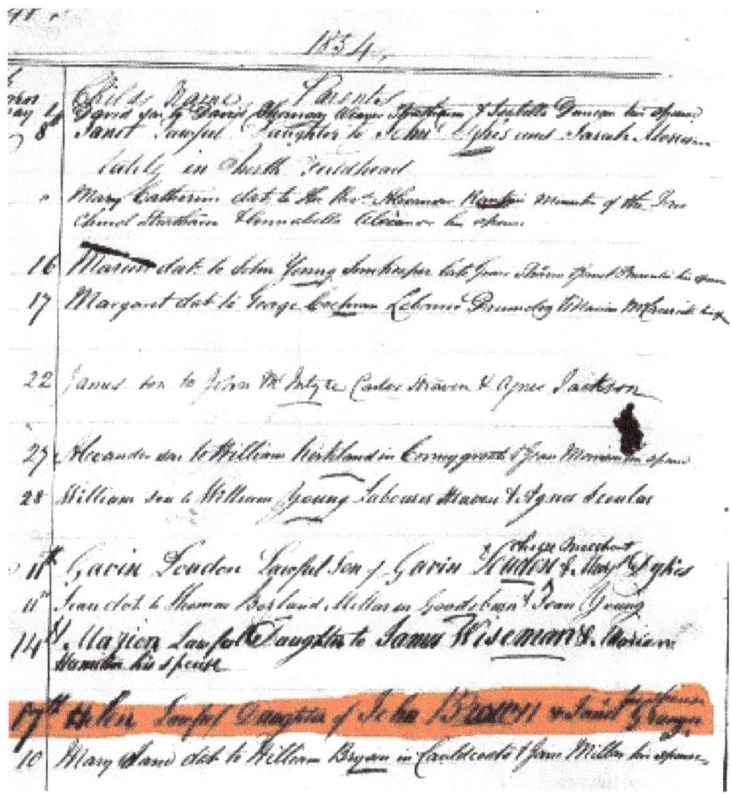

Birth record of Helen Brown, June 17, 1854.
Avondale, Lanarkshire, Scotland.[50]

This unique naming journey adds a layer of intrigue to her life story and highlights the complexity of naming practices and traditions within Scottish culture.

John and Janet, it seems, had little luck when it came to producing sons; in 1857 their sixth daughter Sarah was born. Finally, in 1859 they were overjoyed with the birth of their first son John, followed in 1862 with the birth of their second son Alexander; he was known throughout his life as Sandy. John Jr. would eventually marry Prudence Shipman and Sandy would marry Isabella Wood.

Marriage registration, December 1878,
of Annie Ellen Brown and Thomas Welsh.[51]

John and Janet's eldest daughter, Marion, left home at a young age to help support her family. She was a servant working for the Dykes family on Hazliebank Farm where her father John and uncle Alexander (1827–1868) had worked as young men. Her cousin, James Meikle, worked as a labourer on the same farm.

Countryside in Lanarkshire.[52]

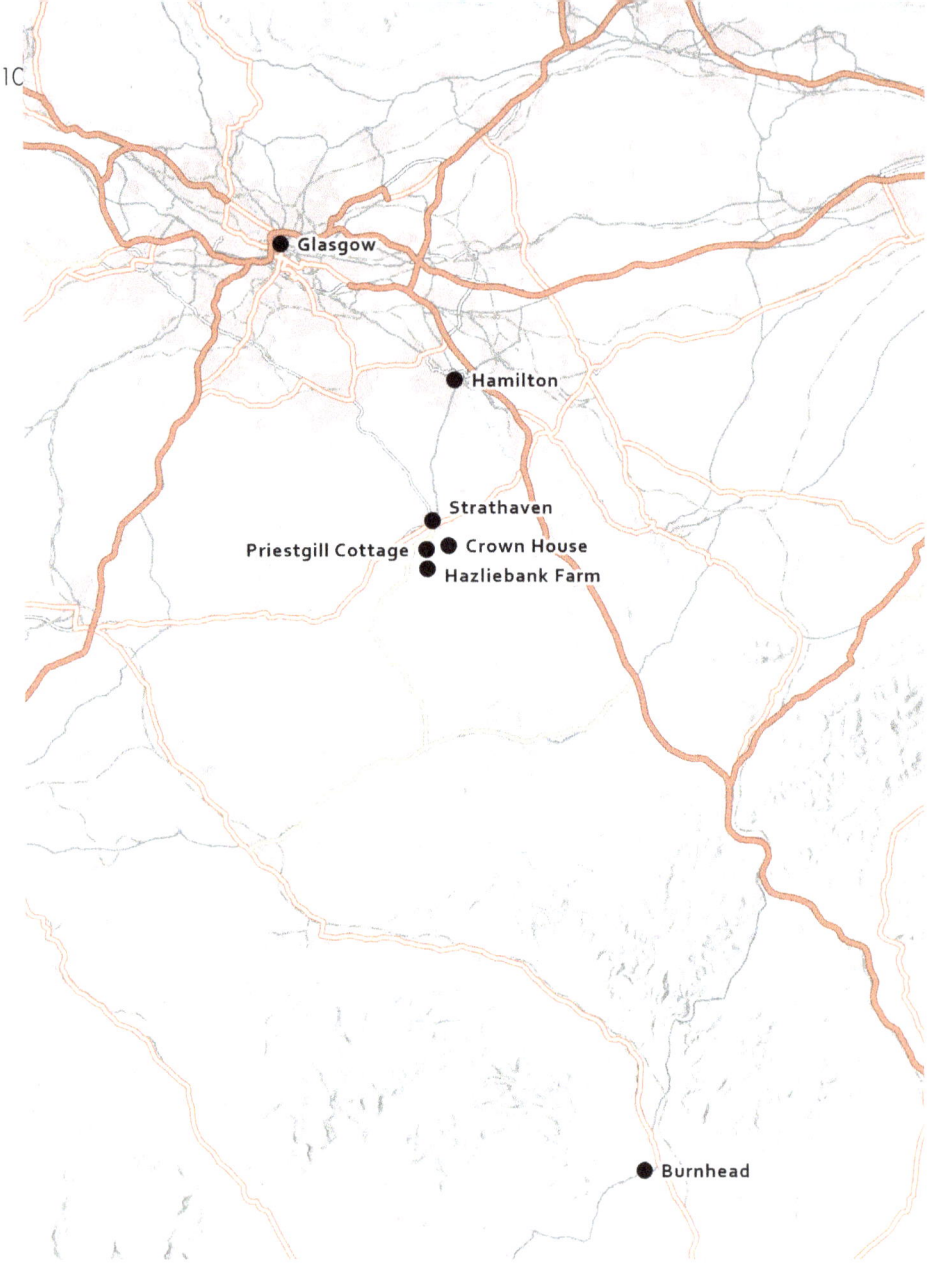

Locations where John Brown (1818–1901) and Janet Granger (1821–?) and their children lived over the years in Scotland.

In 1864, another opportunity for a fresh start arose, and John, Janet, and their family embarked on a journey from Scotland to Upper Canada with hopes of finding a better life. Their decision to seek a new beginning in a distant land would prove to be a monumental one for the entire family.

It would be twenty years after their arrival in Canada, and another move within Canada, before John would realize the dream of land ownership, a significant moment in his life. Through hard work, determination, and perseverance, he carved out a future for his family in this promising new land. John lived a long and productive life, and his presence made a lasting impact right until the modern day.

On November 9, 1901, at the age of eighty-three, John passed away peacefully on St. Joseph Island in Canada at the home of his son Sandy. His death by old age marked the conclusion of a remarkable journey, one filled with diligence, resilience, courage, and an unfailing pursuit of opportunities.

John's legacy would endure through the generations of his descendants as a testament to the enduring spirit and determination that defined his life. His story would forever be interwoven into the tapestry of our family's history, and it would inspire future generations to seize their own opportunities and to strive for the best that life has to offer.

My paternal great-grandmother, Mary Bookman Smith, who lived to be ninety-three, shared with me her memories of John Brown. Her family were neighbours of John's and her first memories of him were when she would have been a young girl of about eleven. Through her eyes, I can almost see him. Her words painted a picture of a stout figure—a man of robust build who possessed a commanding presence. A defining feature that caught her young eyes was his magnificent white beard—to her youthful imagination it brought forth a charming association—John Brown seemed to embody the very essence of Santa Claus! It's a wonderful reminder that our personal stories, shared across time, have the power to kindle feelings of joy and warmth, allowing us to forge a connection with our roots and the people who shaped our legacy.

The Move to Upper Canada

We can't quite be certain when John Brown, the eldest of Duncan Brown and Janet McDonald's children, made the decision to leave Scotland and settle in Upper Canada. Was it something he had dreamed of over the years, or did he, like his grandfather Alexander (1754–?), make a quick decision when opportunity knocked?

He may have heard about the opportunity from friends or possibly even from distant family members who preceded him to the New World. Or maybe he had seen the posters in the various villages encouraging emigration to this bright new colony. All we know is that at some point, John made the conscious decision that the future was more promising for his family in Canada, than it was in his native Scotland.

In Scotland, John and his wife Janet Granger were not wealthy by any means, and their financial prospects were extremely limited. Nearly half of all the land in Scotland was owned by just sixty-eight families, so the chances of John owning land himself were slim. In contrast, land ownership in Canada was made readily available by the government. John and his family would be free of landlord oppression, military service was not required, and taxes were low. John recognized that the move to Canada might very well give him the opportunity of a lifetime and offer a much brighter future for his children.

Poster produced by the Province of Ontario and distributed in the United Kingdom to encourage and entice emigration.[53]

Scots had already been immigrating to the British colonies for years, and between 1815 and 1870, over 170,000 Scots came to Canada. They included highlanders and lowlanders, farmers, teachers, merchants, clergy, and servants.

The British government encouraged Scottish emigration during the nineteenth century to alleviate population pressures and to reduce the burden on social welfare systems. To achieve this, various schemes were developed to transport the "poorer, surplus folk" out of Britain and to resettle them in British North America and other distant colonies of the empire.

These initiatives were supported by government funds or in some cases by private charitable organizations. Nonetheless, some Scots financed their own migration and resettlement. As a tenant farmer, John Brown did not have any land to sell to help finance moving his family. Although it is not clear if he received assistance, it is highly unlikely that he financed his family's entire resettlement to Upper Canada on his own. Given the cost of moving a family of nine, it's more likely that they pooled their meager resources and received some assistance to make their way to Canada.

The Province of Ontario produced an information pamphlet for potential emigrants that provided details about crown lands, agriculture, commerce, religion, cost of living, and wages, among other things.

Should an emigrant be considering a possible move to the United States, numerous comparisons outlined why a move to Canada would be the more advantageous decision. The circular gave inducements to emigrate to Canada not simply for the good wages and cheap living in the company of kindred people in a naturally rich country possessing a pleasant and healthy climate—but for the confident prospect that even the poorest man could become a possessor of the soil, earning a good living for himself while settling his children comfortably. Many rich and independent farmers all over Upper Canada had been poor immigrant labourers without any means whatever just a few years before. All of this certainly painted a perfect picture.

The British government created advertising programs to encourage people to settle in Ontario. Ontario was referred to at the time as Upper Canada. With pamphlets, posters, and very persuasive agents, emigrants were drawn to Ontario for the free land and with hope for a better future.[54]

However, an opinion piece published in the Glasgow Herald in 1862 painted a far less rosy picture. It described a more realistic image of what lay ahead should one have the courage to emigrate to Canada. The author advised that large families and anyone with a delicate constitution should not emigrate. If someone was a "ne'er-do-well," Canada was not the place for them. Life would most likely be unsuitable and miserable for women and children there.

On the other hand, any rough and ready bachelors who loved the wild and the speculative life would be well suited to the challenges offered by Canada. If a man could bring sufficient funds, he could build a rough shanty, clear the land, shoot, fish, and hunt deer; after a few years, he might see sufficient income from his agricultural pursuits to independently support himself.

The ordinary Scotsman would find the severity of the Canadian climate very harsh: extreme cold—and heat in the summer approaching that of the tropics. The emigrant would need to have will, muscles of iron, and be a jack of all trades. If he believed he would attain immediate wealth, he would be sadly mistaken. (Although the article doesn't mention it, blackflies and mosquitos were also of great concern.)

It is apparent that John Brown didn't read this article or that he chose to ignore the advice. He and his family were headed to Canada. Opportunity was knocking, and he was ready to answer that appealing tone.

In May 1864, John, Janet, and their seven children prepared themselves for a life-changing several-week journey aboard an Allan Line ship that would be departing from Glasgow and had Quebec as its destination.

The family consisted of John the patriarch aged forty-six, his wife Janet forty-three, and their children: Marion twenty-one, Jessie nineteen, Mary thirteen, Helen/Ellen ten, Sarah seven, John five, and the youngest, Alexander "Sandy," aged two.

Leaving behind their homeland, extended family, and friends, the Browns would face an uncertain future filled with unimaginable challenges. Despite the difficulties that lay ahead, they approached their journey with courage and determination.

On the day of their departure, the docks were bustling with activity as hundreds of emigrants gathered to get onboard. The air was filled with noise, commotion, and a sense of both excitement and apprehension. There was a flurry of activity; people were shouting, carts lined the dock area which was now piled high with trunks and crates. Those same trunks and crates were bursting with the essentials that people thought they would need for the journey—and also what they thought they would need upon their arrival in Canada.

Amidst the chaos, there was a constant stream of people moving back and forth, trying to ensure that they were in the right place to board their ship. Families clung together, anxious not to be separated.

The Browns' journey was not aboard a luxury liner, but an Allan Line steam ship that was used to transport mail and about three hundred steerage passengers. The shipping company had been established in 1819, with the Canadian subsidiary, the Montreal Ocean Steamship Company being established in 1854.

The line covered transatlantic routes between ports in the United Kingdom (Glasgow, Londonderry, Liverpool, and London) to North American ports. Canadian ports included Quebec, Montreal, and Halifax. St. John's, Newfoundland was also one of the ports of call. By the 1880s, the Allan Line would become the world's largest privately owned shipping company.

Crowds of passengers wait to board ships on the docks in Glasgow.[55]

Over the years the Allan Line lost eight ships in Canadian waters. A dark reminder of how perilous sea travel was, even in the nineteenth century.

Contractual obligations with the Canadian government to deliver mail and the associated penalties when there were delays may have been a contributory cause of the losses, as the captains often chose speed over safety. Regardless of the cause, the transatlantic journey was only the first of many challenges that the Brown family would face and overcome in their move to Canada.

ALLAN LINE
Royal Mail Service to Canada.

The Steamers of this Line are commanded by navigators of acknowledged ability, who have by long and faithful service proved themselves worthy of the confidence and esteem of their employers, and they are assisted in the navigation of the ships by thoroughly trained and experienced officers.

THE STEAMERS ARE DESPATCHED AS FOLLOWS :—

LIVERPOOL, GLASGOW, LONDONDERRY, and QUEENSTOWN to CANADA (Quebec, Halifax, &c.) Every Week throughout the year.

FARES :—Saloon, 12 to 21 Guineas.
Return Tickets, available for Twelve Months £25 and £30.
INTERMEDIATE, £8.   STEERAGE, at low Rates.
Special Through Rates to Inland Points.

THE ALLAN LINE ILLUSTRATED GUIDE, embracing particulars of "Summer Tours" and "Round Trip" Tickets, distributed free to applicants.

The Steamers of this Line afford the greatest amount of comfort to all classes of Passengers, being furnished with every modern improvement.

The voyage to Quebec has distinguished recommendations as compared with the other routes to the American Continent. From land to land the average passage is not more than six days. Once within the Straits of Belle Isle, ocean travelling is over, and for hundreds of miles the steamer proceeds, first through the Gulf and then through the magnificent River St. Lawrence. This is an immense advantage.

☞ ASSISTED PASSAGES TO CANADA are Granted to Mechanics, Navvies, Agricultural and General Labourers, and their Families, and to Female Domestic Servants.

☞ Application for Assisted Passages to be made upon the Special Forms which are provided for the purpose.

Poster produced by the Allan Shipping Line.[56]

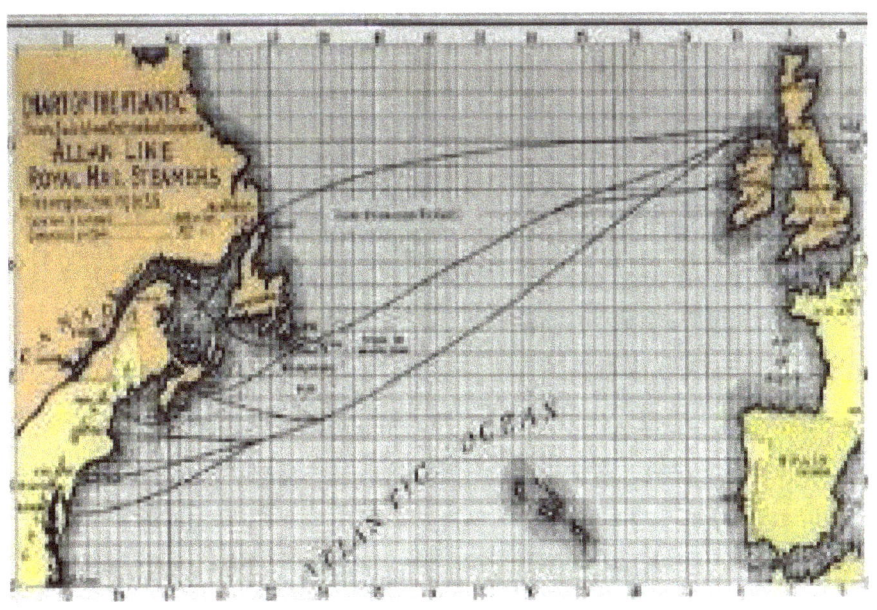

Allan Line steamship.[57]

Allan Line mail steamer routes from Britain
to Canada and the United States.[58]

Once all the passengers and cargo were on board, the ship carrying John Brown and his family departed the port in Glasgow and navigated the River Clyde out to the Firth of Clyde. Heading west, they travelled through the North Channel, which separates the rugged coasts of Scotland and Ireland, and then steamed out to the open Atlantic Ocean.

This part of the journey was about five hundred nautical miles and could take between two and three days. Some passengers would succumb to sea sickness even before entering the Atlantic Ocean. It took some time for passengers to get their sea legs. Children it would seem were less affected, running about and laughing at their inability to stay on their feet. As they sailed towards their new life, John and his family clung to hope and to the belief that their future held promise, even in the face of the unknown.

The type of vessel that the Browns were on was seldom comfortable. Overcrowding, bad provisioning, and sanitation problems were complicated by the increasing presence of diseases such as smallpox and cholera. Passengers carried all their belongings in a wooden trunk with a maximum weight allowed of eighteen pounds, and they were required to supply their own bedding and cooking utensils. Families were given supplies each week to meet their nutritional requirements: 3½ lb. of bread, 3½ lb. of oatmeal, 2½ lb. of flour, 2 lb. of potatoes, ½ lb. of sugar, 1½ lb. of beef, 2 oz. of tea, 1 lb. of pork, 1 lb. of sugar, 2 oz. of salt, ½ oz. of mustard, ¼ oz. of pepper, 1 gill of vinegar, and each day were provided 3 quarts of water.

There was a communal area of about twelve feet by six feet

for everyone to use to organize their meals. Often, the Browns only managed to get one meal prepared in a day; they had to spend too much time waiting in line while they braced their feet when the ship rolled and heaved. An inspector on the ship was noted as saying, "If the steerage passengers act like cattle at meals, it is undoubtedly because they are treated as such."

Like the other steerage passengers, the Brown family began their day by cleaning their own berths and then trying to find an opportunity to prepare their breakfast amongst the hundreds of other passengers.

If the weather was good, the passengers would be allowed on deck for a limited amount of time each day, usually for a few hours in the morning and a few hours in the afternoon. They would often see passing ships in the distance and the occasional whale spouting. During periods of bad weather, passengers were confined to their quarters below deck—sometimes for days at a time—with limited access to fresh air and exercise.

John Brown and his family did not fare well on this journey. They ran short of food, and John fell on board the ship and broke his arm. This left his wife Janet in a state of distress, desperately pondering how they would cope as they sailed on into the unknown.

The passage to Canada was difficult and dangerous and, depending on the weather, could take up to six weeks. Once the ship that John and his family were sailing on had crossed the Atlantic, it needed to navigate the Gulf of St. Lawrence.

It would then need to steam up the St. Lawrence River from Rimouski to Montreal. This was nearly 270 nautical miles.

Some fresh air on the deck.[59]

In the Gulf of St. Lawrence, the hazards were perhaps even greater than the Atlantic itself. As their voyage was in the spring, the crew would have to navigate through snowstorms and ice. Also, iron deposits in the vicinity of the St. Lawrence aggravated the compass. The river was badly lit, and not all maritime pilots had sufficient experience to take charge of a large steamship under these conditions. There was also a series of sunken reefs, shoals, and flats, all improperly mapped. To make matters worse, the tide did not run true, and the channel was often very narrow. It was said that crossing the Atlantic was child's play compared with the voyage on the St. Lawrence to Montreal.

As the ship ventured deeper into the expanse of the Gulf of St. Lawrence, passengers caught glimpses of playful porpoises swimming alongside the ship while land birds circled above. Then suddenly, the cry of "Land!" echoed throughout the ship. John and his family, along with the other passengers, rushed to the rail and were captivated by the sight of enchanting small islands, picturesque lighthouses, and flourishing farms along the riverbank.

The panoramic view continued to unfold, revealing groves of majestic trees, charming towns, and magnificent churches with towering spires.

As nightfall descended, the distant glow of shimmering lights emanating from the windows of far-off houses added a touch of magic to the spectacle. After enduring countless days of relentless rolling seas, this breathtaking vista proved to be a long-awaited respite for all on board.

Navigating the St. Lawrence River.[60]

Before John, Janet, and their children could start their new lives, the ship was required to anchor at Grosse Île. This was an immigration depot that had opened in 1832 (it operated until 1937), and it was located in the St. Lawrence River, about forty-eight kilometers northeast of Quebec City.

If there were any sick passengers on board, a blue flag would have been raised, and ill passengers would have been taken ashore to go into quarantine. The remainder of the passengers would then have been disembarked, processed, and housed either in sheds with berths or, in some cases, back on the ship.

Grosse Île quarantine post.[61]

There was great commotion and excitement among the passengers at being back on dry land once again. Large copper kettles were set up with plenty of water and firewood for those that wished to wash their clothes. Some took the opportunity to stroll around the island, feeling the fresh air and solid ground beneath their feet. Once cleared, the ship was sent on to Quebec City, and finally, to Montreal.

The Browns then began the second leg of their journey to reach their final destination—Middlesex County near London, Ontario. It is more than likely that they took a train from Montreal to Toronto or Hamilton and then a second train to London, but the exact details of their trek has been lost to time.

In Montreal, John, Janet, and their children were encouraged to proceed as quickly as possible to their destination, either via train or by steam ship. If they required assistance or direction, they were to only request it from the official, listed government agents, as there were unscrupulous people taking advantage of the newcomers by charging a fee for their services. Con men and scammers are apparently nothing new.

They were advised to use caution before agreeing to pay for passage, as there was great competition between railway and shipping companies. The cost of travel from Quebec to London, Ontario by railway or steamer was $12.55 for first class and $5.85 for second class. The Brown family of nine travelling second class would have had to pay about $53 Canadian dollars for their passage to London. That would be the equivalent of just over $1,000 today.

Finally, after a long and arduous journey, the Browns arrived at their new home in Middlesex County, Ontario. Right away, the four oldest girls, Marion, Janet, Ellen, and Mary, were sent out as domestic servants to help with the family expenses. They earned fifty cents a month, a modest but typical wage for domestic work at the time. Scottish girls were highly regarded for their shrewdness, piety, and incomparable work ethic, making them sought-after candidates for domestic service positions.

As such, the girls likely had no difficulty in securing employment. Their commitment to their work and dedication to their employers would have been highly valued, and they would have been expected to uphold their reputation as hardworking and trustworthy Scottish girls.

The youngest daughter, Sarah, aged about eight, and the boys John and Sandy, ages six and two, were too young to be sent out to work. Sarah and John did attend some school, as did Sandy when he became old enough.

They found a strong Scots community when they arrived, as Middlesex County and other nearby counties were home to more than two thousand Scottish immigrants by 1861. This eclectic community included artisans, ministers, farmers, and teachers who had left their homeland for a variety of reasons. These were people who enjoyed the comradery of other Scots and who were willing to help the newcomers as much as they could.

The most likely place to get that feeling of home was their Presbyterian church. The church provided a strong blend of social, spiritual, and ethnic support where Scottish immigrants could be themselves, including of course in the use of their traditional Gaelic language.

With everyone working together and supporting one another, it didn't take long for John and his family to get established in their new home. It is more than likely that he had made inquiries and had secured a farm to rent prior to their departure from Scotland, since land grants were few and far between in this area. John rented fifty acres (Lot 27, 3rd Concession) in the Township of Nissouri West in Middlesex County, near St. Marys, Ontario.

Over the next seven years, John worked hard on the farm, cultivating about three acres of gardens and an apple orchard.

He was farming wheat, barley, oats, peas, corn, potatoes, and hay. There was also pasture for livestock. This was sufficient to feed his own family, with the remainder generating some income to pay the rent and to keep the farm running.

At this point he owned two oxen, two cows, seventeen sheep, and five pigs and he was able to sell butter, animals for slaughter, wool, and firewood. His wife Janet and the older girls did some weaving, and they were able to sell cloth to supplement their income. Everyone worked together toward a common goal.

The Canadian County Atlas Digital Project

Full record for Brown, John

Last Name	Brown
First Name	John
Post Office	St. Ives
Township	Nissouri West
County	Middlesex
Atlas Date	1878

Concession and Lot	Lot Size
II, 37	50

John Brown rental property, 3rd Concession, Nissouri West Township, Middlesex County, Ontario, Canada.[62]

The income that the family earned during these early years—along with their skills and experience—would pave the way for one more move within Ontario—a move that would allow them in time to become landowners.

Marion Granger Brown (1843–1930) A Dream Come True

Marion Granger Brown.

On July 8, 1868, four years after John, Janet, and family arrived in Canada, eldest daughter, Marion, married John Henry, ten years her senior. Her sister Mary was her witness and John and Janet's next-door neighbour, Presbyterian Minister Robert Hall, conducted the ceremony. John Henry had arrived from Scotland around the same time as the Browns. After their marriage, Marion and John purchased fifty acres, Lot 27 on the 4th Concession of Nissouri West, not far from Marion's parents and near the small village of Wellburn, about ten kilometers from St. Marys, Ontario.

It was a good area for farming, especially for dairy farming. There was a post office, general store, blacksmith, and a cheese factory in the village. Marion and John had a good team of horses, four cows, fourteen sheep, and two pigs—and they even kept bees. They grew spring wheat, barley, oats, and peas and had two acres of garden and an orchard. They lived on the farm until John Henry's death in 1915 at the age of eighty-two. Marion then moved to live with her daughter Jessie until her death in 1930 at age eighty-seven.

Marion accomplished what her parents had dreamed of for their children: she had six strapping sons and two daughters who were all property owners and well educated. Four of her sons moved to the United States. William and Albert, along with her two daughters, Jessie and Marion, remained in the area and farmed for many years. They took advantage of opportunities just like their great-great-grandfather Alexander (1754–?) and grandfather John (1818–1901), pursuing a dream that never faded.

The Canadian County Atlas Digital Project	
Full record for Henry, John	
Last Name	Henry
First Name	John
Post Office	Belton
Township	Nissouri West
County	Middlesex
Atlas Date	1878
Concession and Lot	Lot size

John and Marion Henry property, 4th Concession, Nissouri West Township, Middlesex County, Ontario, Canada.[63]

Marion Brown and John Henry's sons. (left to right) William, Simon, George, John, James, Albert.

Jessie Louisa Henry (1883–1966). Daughter of Marion Brown and John Henry.

Marion Mable Henry (1886–1964). Daughter
of Marion Brown and John Henry.

John Henry and Marion Brown. North Nissouri Presbyterian Cemetery.[64]

Janet "Jessie" Brown (1845–1876)
Just a Short Time

Daughter Janet, or "Jessie" as she was called, was the next of John and Janet Brown's daughters to marry. On February 11, 1873, Jessie married John McLarty, who was also from Scotland naturally enough. They were married by the same minister Robert Hall as her sister Marion and John Henry had been—and again— sister Mary was a witness. John McLarty was employed by the Great Western Railway as a fireman and later as an engineer. Jessie and John lived in London, Ontario, enjoying the town life, unlike their more rural relations.

Great Western Railway locomotive (1860s).[65]

In 1874, Jessie and John had a daughter, Agnes "Mary" named after John's mother. Two years later, Jessie became very ill and on May 10, 1876, she died of hydrocephalus (water on the brain) at just thirty-one years of age. She was buried in Woodland Cemetery in London, Ontario. Her daughter, Agnes "Mary", was just two years old at the time.

Reverend Robert Hall, neighbour to the Browns.
He conducted the weddings of Marion and Janet Brown.[66]

Janet Brown McLarty May 10, 1876, and her mother-in-law
Agnes McLarty. Woodlawn Cemetery London, Ontario.[67]

John McLarty remarried a short time later to Margaret "Maggie" Baille, and they went on to have five children, two of whom died. William, age five, died of diphtheria and Douglas, age one, died of bronchitis. Sadly, child mortality was common in those days, before the advent of modern medicine and antibiotics.

Agnes "Mary" lived with her father and stepmother until her early twenties, when she moved to Michigan, where she married William Harmon in 1902. They came back to Ontario for a short time but returned to Michigan, where Agnes "Mary" died in 1948 at the age of seventy-three.

Jessie's new life in Canada had been short. Only twelve years after her arrival, her life had ended tragically. After all her family's struggles and triumphs, Jessie had not had the opportunity to live a full life, to reap the benefits of what Canada had to offer, and to experience what other members of her family did.

Helen "Ellen" Annie Brown (1854-1943)
Last Survivor

Next to marry was John and Janet's daughter Helen "Ellen", and it was on her marriage registration that she added the name "Annie." It seems that Ellen may have had her first child, Frederick, in 1876, prior to her marriage to Thomas Welsh on December 30, 1878, in Port Huron, Michigan. Thomas was born in New York in 1852 and was of Irish descent. Ellen and Thomas lived their entire lives in Port Huron, St. Clair County, Michigan. Thomas was employed as a maritime engineer, and he plied the Great Lakes for more than forty years until his retirement. He died in 1917 at age sixty-four.

Shortly after his death, Ellen moved in with her daughter Bessie and her family. Sadly, Bessie died in 1937 at the age of just fifty-six. Ellen was then welcomed into her daughter Mary's home until Ellen's death on December 26, 1943, at the age of eighty-nine. Ellen outlived two of her children and all her siblings. She is buried in the Lakeside Cemetery in Port Huron, Michigan and was the last survivor of the family of nine who had bravely boarded the ship to Canada in 1864.

Funerals—

Mrs. Ellen Welsh

Funeral services for Mrs. Ellen Welsh, 89, member of a prominent Port Huron pioneer family and resident of Port Huron 68 years, who died Sunday in the home of her daughter, Mrs. Earl Madill, 809 Beard street, after a long illness, were held this afternoon in the Kipp funeral home. Rev. N. S. Sichterman, pastor of First Presbyterian church, officiated.

E. B. Busby, Grosse Pointe Farms; George W. Brunton, Kenmore, N. Y.; Edward C. Welsh, Chicago, Ill.; and William T. Welsh, City Treasurer Earl Madill and W. W. Shindle, all of Port Huron, were pallbearers. Burial was in Lakeside cemetery.

Times Herald, Port Huron, Michigan. December 29, 1943.

The Big Flittin—Another Island

T he Scottish word "flit" means to move house, and that's exactly what John Brown (1818–1901), his daughters Mary and Sarah and sons, John and Sandy, did after about fourteen years in Nissouri Township, where John had been renting fifty acres of farmland. Once again, opportunity knocked, and John Brown was determined to answer it.

Sometime between 1871 and 1877, John Brown's wife Janet passed away. Even after nearly forty years of searching, I have not been able to find a death or burial record that I can definitively confirm for Janet. I know that she did not accompany her husband and children to St. Joseph Island in 1878, and on the next census held in 1881, John Brown indicates that he was a widower.

The reason for John's "big flittin" was to take advantage of the Free Grants and Homestead Act that the government had established in 1868. The Act encouraged farmers in southern Ontario, which is where John lived, to relocate to Algoma, which is a district located near Lake Huron and the North Channel. If they made the move, the head of each household would be provided with up to two hundred acres of land—an opportunity that John viewed as too good to pass up. Individuals were encouraged to contact government agent John Bowker in Bruce Mines, Ontario as he had sixty thousand acres at his disposal under the Free Grants and Homestead Act.

While "free" was in the name of the act, recipients did have to meet specific criteria to gain their land grant, which was known as receiving their land patent. Within the first five years of arriving on the land that they wanted, they had to clear and cultivate fifteen acres for each grant and build a dwelling of at least sixteen feet by twenty feet. They would then have to live there continuously and pay a modest application fee. Once all the requirements were satisfied, a patent would be issued, and the land would be placed in the name of the applicant.

This meant that John Sr., John Jr., and Sandy would need to work together to clear enough space for three grants (two for John Sr. and one for John Jr.) and they would need to build and occupy three structures.

John and his children were up for the challenge. In November 1878, John sold all his livestock; this provided much-needed funds for his family's journey north to St. Joseph Island. It is likely that they waited until late in the year to ensure that they could harvest and sell their remaining crops before embarking on their trip. Their journey began by boarding the Grand Trunk Railway in St. Marys. Their first destination was Collingwood which was a major transfer point for both goods and passengers between the railway and ships.

Steamships had been navigating the Great Lakes since 1816, and the Western Advertiser of London, Ontario, community networks and government publications had been specifically highlighting the desirability of St. Joseph Island and the North Shore for settlement. Steamers from Sarnia, Collingwood, and

Owen Sound transported a significant number of settlers who were making their way to Marksville (Hilton Beach), Richards Landing, and Bruce Mines.

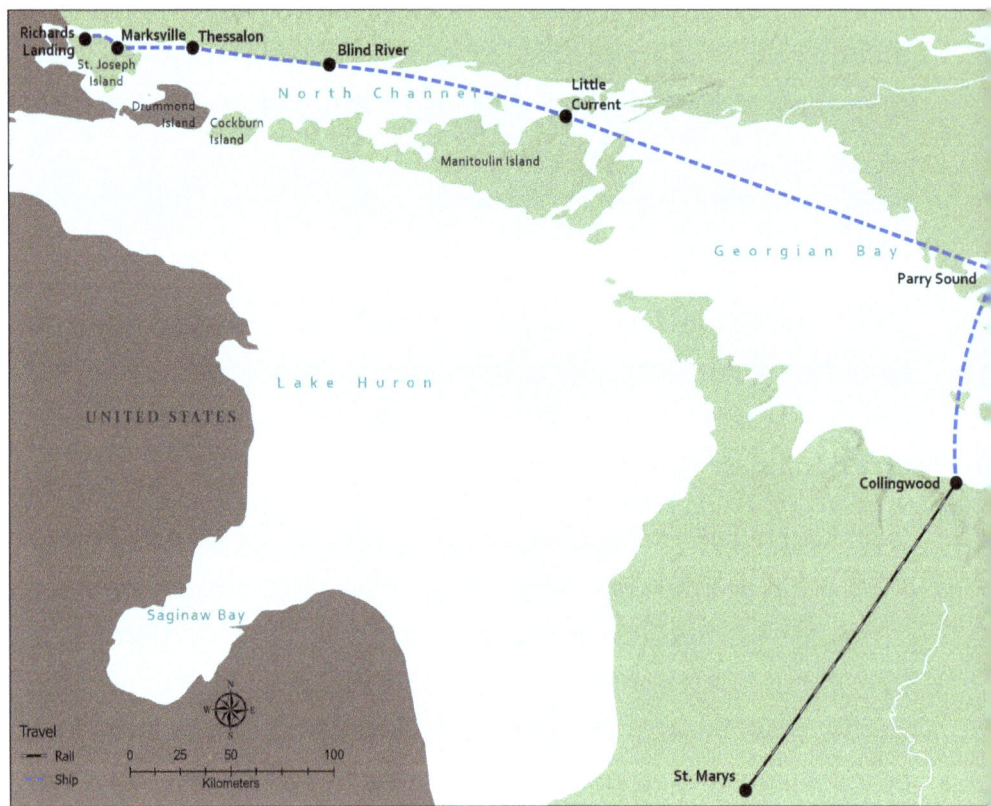

Journey To St. Joseph Island.

Among the many steamships that journeyed to the Island and North Shore during this time period were the Waubuno, Northern Belle, and Northern Queen.

Upon reaching Collingwood, John and his extended family boarded one of these lake steamers, beginning their journey along the eastern part of Georgian Bay. The steamer then navigated the narrows at Little Current on Manitoulin Island then made several stops along the North Shore. The scenic route featured striking rocky outcroppings, wind-swept islands, and iconic white pine trees that continue to captivate travelers to this day.

Although the voyage was shorter than their trip from Scotland, it was not without its perils, particularly due to the cold and unpredictable weather at that time of year. The Great Lakes in the wintertime are not to be trifled with. Throughout the years, numerous steamers were lost, wrecked, or destroyed by fire and storms, highlighting the dangers of these maritime travels.

Wind swept islands of Georgian Bay.[68]

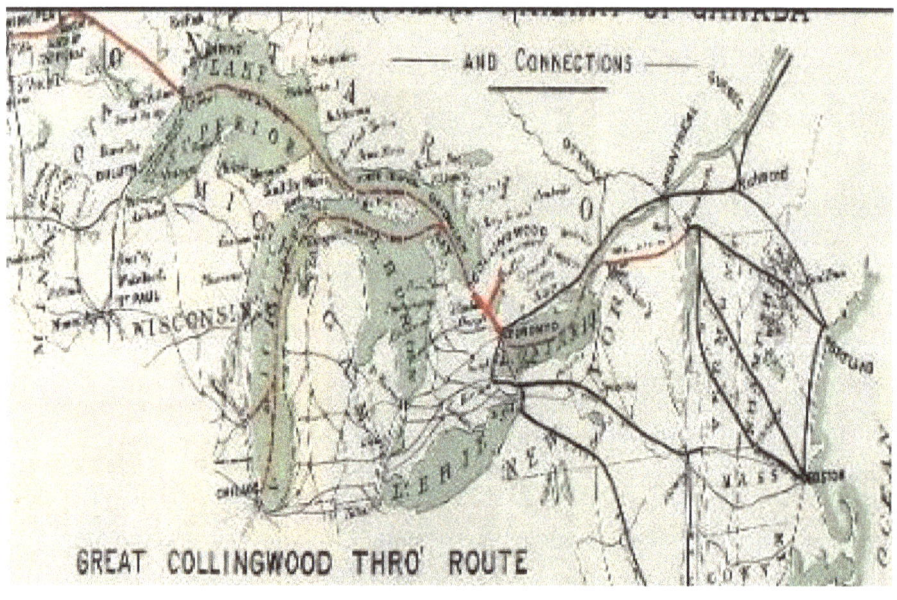

Grand Trunk Railway station St. Marys, Ontario.[69]

Rail and ship connections for Canada and the United States
—through or around the Great Lakes.[70]

Northern Belle. [71]

Name	*Northern Belle*
Owner	Georgian Bay Navigation Company
Completed	1875
Out of Service	1898-11-10
Fate	Overwhelmed by an internal fire in Byng Inlet, Georgian Bay
Notes	Formerly Gladys

Advertisement in the Northern Advance, June 20, 1878.[72]

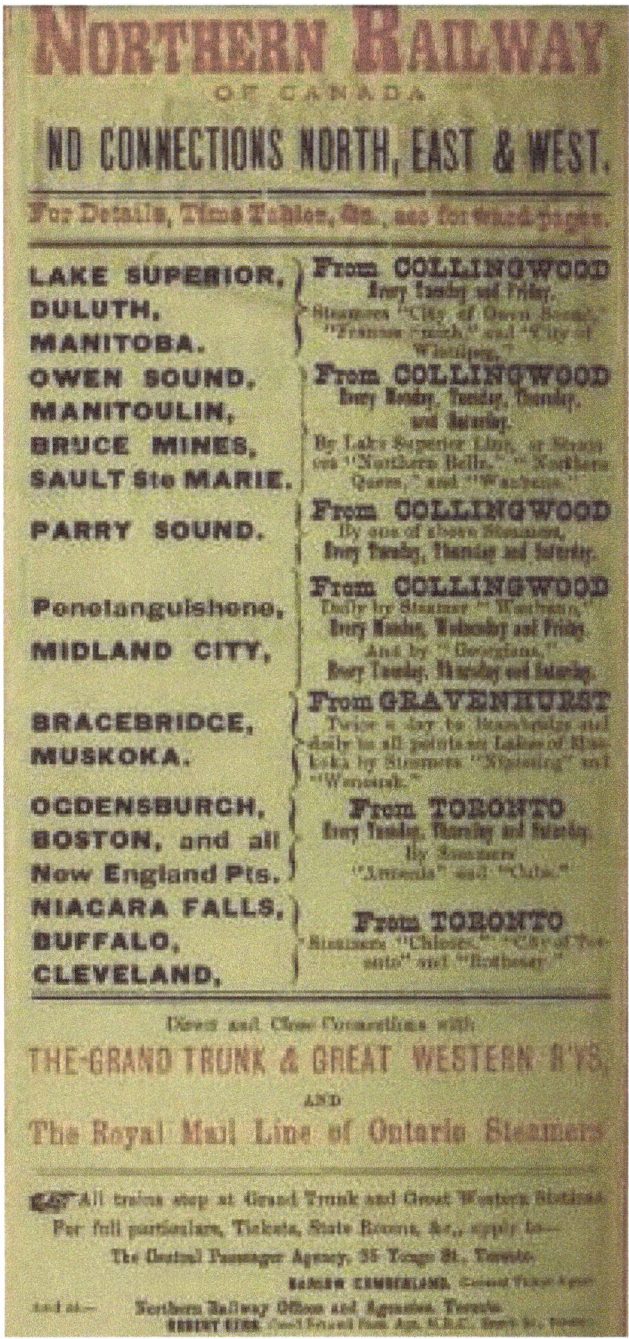

Timetable for Northern Railway.[73]

Government Dock, Richards Landing, Ont.

The Richards Landing dock—the place where the Browns arrived on St. Joseph Island.[74]

As they approached their new island home, John noted the stark contrast between his birthplace of Easdale Island and St. Joseph Island. St. Joseph Island is a sprawling expanse, and it dwarfs the modest size of Easdale Island, a barren rock with very few trees. The lush greenery of St. Joseph Island, densely populated with hardwood, paints a vastly different picture than the rugged barren landscape of Easdale Island.

St. Joseph Island is the third largest island on the Great Lakes, and it played an important role in the early fur trade and as a staging point for the first victory for British North America in the War of 1812. Between 1874 and 1882, there was a great influx of settlers, many from the London, Ontario (Middlesex County) area; these included John Brown and his family.

Hamilton Bay south east shore of St. Joseph Island.[75]

Roads, schools, and churches were being built. The village of Richards Landing on the island was becoming a commercial hub, as was the village of Marksville, which was later renamed Hilton Beach.

The island encompasses nearly ninety thousand acres, with the highest point being referred to as "The Mountain" at 345 meters; that was where the Browns would eventually settle. Easdale Island is about sixty-two acres with the highest point being just thirty-eight meters above sea level.

In a promotional pamphlet put out by the Province of Ontario, Mr. George Hamilton, crown land agent, who was living in Richards Landing, noted that one whole concession on St. Joseph Island was settled by individuals from the London, Ontario area. He quoted comments from four farmers living on the island who had come from Middlesex County, Ontario, and they described this as fine farming country and a sportsman's paradise—abounding with all kinds of game and fish.

They noted that the land was fertile; you could grow grain of all kinds and the very best fruits in a very agreeable climate. Cattle and sheep were reported to do very well on the island as well. The island offered something for every need and taste.

So, it would seem that John Brown had made the right decision when he had decided to settle on St. Joseph Island. However, to truly succeed, there was much work to be done.

Enjoying the green grass on St. Joe.[76]

Mary Brown (1851–1939)
Home At Last

Mary Brown.

On May 9, 1879—which was not long after the Browns arrived on St. Joseph Island—John and Janet's daughter Mary married Richard Fisher in Bruce Mines. There was quite an age difference, with Mary being twenty-seven and Richard forty-six. The Fisher family had arrived in Bruce Mines years before with their six sons and two daughters. The boys worked in the copper mine and the girls were seamstresses. Richard was only thirteen years old when they arrived in Canada, but he was an experienced miner having worked in the mines in Scotland since the age of ten.

Mary and Richard settled on St. Joseph Island with her father John, sister Sarah, and brothers John and Sandy who stayed with them for a time. The couple had five children, Janet (who was known as Jessie), Richard (known as Garfield), Catherine, George, and Sarah, all of whom remained in Algoma District.

Mary's first pregnancy did not go well. In 1880 when daughter Jessie was born, she was so tiny that she was wrapped in wool and carried on a pillow for three months. Mary was not strong enough to look after her. A teacher, Miss McKinnon—who boarded with the family—looked after baby Jessie and Mary until she recovered her strength.

Jessie Fisher (1880–1974). Born St. Joseph Island—daughter of Mary Brown (1851-1939) and Richard Fisher (1833-1903).

Richard Fisher died in 1903 at age seventy-one and is buried in the Grace United Cemetery in Hilton Beach.

By this time, the population of St. Joseph Island had reached about three thousand. Word was that the farms there were beautiful, like no others in the province. There were two sawmills, four general stores, schools, three churches, and a blacksmith shop. The lumber trade was booming and there was daily steamship service. Hay and grain crops were above average, and the apples and other produce would have done credit to any country.

Bridge to St. Joseph Island completed in 1972.

The island had good roads, beautiful scenery, a healthy and invigorating climate, and its land was fertile and cheap. The St. Joseph council had discussed sending a delegation to the

Ontario Legislature to lobby politicians to build a bridge. Residents at the time complained that politicians had made promises, but no bridge had been forthcoming. Requests and opinions fell on deaf ears, it seems, as it took another seventy years before a bridge was finally built from the mainland to St. Joseph Island.

After Richard's death, Mary remained in their home, and in 1911 her children, Janet "Jessie," Richard "Garfield," and Sarah were living with her. Neither Richard "Garfield" nor George ever married, and Garfield lived with his mother Mary until her death in 1939 at the age of eighty-eight. Mary is also buried in the Grace United Cemetery.

St. Joseph Island is surrounded by ice for most of the winter, creating a frozen roadway that residents often used to travel to the mainland and other nearby islands. This routine, however, was not without risk. On the day of Mary's funeral, a near tragedy unfolded when her daughter Catherine and family became disoriented on the ice during a storm while returning to their home on Portlock Island. Lost on the ice for about three hours during the storm, they eventually found the shore and took refuge at the Fisher home for the night before resuming their journey the following day. Disaster was narrowly averted.

Sarah Brown (1857–1936)
Heartache and Resilience

Sarah Brown.

I n 1880, Sarah, the youngest daughter of John Brown and Janet Granger, married John George Kirk, sixteen years her senior. He was a happy and cheerful man and was well liked. A member of the Free Methodist Church, he also served on the first board of trustees for the Mountain School, serving alongside his brother-in-law, Sandy Brown.

John Kirk had come to Canada from Ireland with his first wife Margaret Dogsleau. They had settled in Quebec, where their son John George Kirk II had been born in 1856. Records indicate that they did not speak French, so they opted to make the move to Elderslie in southwestern Ontario.

London Asylum for the Insane.[77]

Tragedy seemed to follow the Kirk family. In 1871 it is noted that both John George Kirk's first wife, Margaret Dogsleau, and his sister, Fanny Kirk, were not of sound mind. Margaret died on February 11, 1876 in the London Asylum for the Insane. The cause of death was chronic dysentery. Fanny died in 1879 of tuberculosis, and it was noted that she had been an invalid for several years.

But their tragic tale didn't end there. John George Kirk II's, first wife drowned in 1898 in Burk's Falls. John George Kirk II's son William took his own life in 1927, and a year later in 1928, John George II and his second wife Elise Baillod died in a car accident in California.

Now living on St. Joseph Island and married to Sarah Brown, John Kirk received his land patent in 1883 from the Crown. He had fulfilled the settlement requirements and was granted one hundred acres on Lot 9, Concession L, which he and Sarah farmed.

John George Kirk II.

WOMAN DROWNED.

Burk's Falls, May 3.—Mrs. George Kirk, wife of the foreman in the yard department of the tannery here, launched out in a flat-bottomed boat, which she propelled by means of a paddle, seated at the stern end. Crossing the river she glided down past the tannery with the aid of the current and her paddle at a fairly good rate of speed. When about 200 yards below the tannery her husband, who was parading the opposite bank of the river in the same direction, heard the boat strike a log or snag, which precipitated Mrs. Kirk into the river with a splash. She screamed for help, but Mr. Kirk, being unable to swim, and having no boat at hand, could render no assistance. She soon sank in eight feet of water.

Ottawa Citizen May 3, 1898.

Unfortunately, John Kirk's second family, with Sarah, also had its misfortunes. In 1886 their son, George Albert, died of hydrocephalus (water on the brain) just a week after his birth. Son John Alexander "Alex" or "Lex" moved to Michigan and served in the First World War. He married Marie Kruase in 1917 and for a time made his living as a mason for a building contractor.

Oil Man Killed as Earthquake Shakes Derrick

BAKERSFIELD, July 8. (Exclusive) Richard Kirk, 37 years of age, of Taft, tool dresser for the Lakeview Oil Company, was fatally injured last night when an earthquake shook the rig on which he was working, dislodging a heavy timber in the top of the derrick and crushing his skull.

Kirk, according to a special dispatch received here today from Taft, was splicing a cable in the Lakeview No. 2 well, two miles north of Maricopa on the Taft-Maricopa Highway, when the earthquake struck. Tearing loose with a crash, the heavy timber dropped more than fifty feet, striking the oil worker with terrific force. He was rushed to a Taft hospital, but died almost instantly.

Kirk was well known on the west side, where he had resided several years. He leaves his mother, Mrs. Sarah Kirk, 1035 Wood street, South Taft.

Accidental death of Richard Kirk. Los Angeles Daily, July 8, 1927.

In September 1928, he was diagnosed with leukemia, and he died just two months later at the young age of forty-five. Sarah and John's youngest son Richard, also known as Emerson, moved to California, and worked for the Lakeview Oil Company, where he was fatally injured. He died in 1927 at age thirty-six when, due to aftershocks from an earthquake, a load of timber fell and crushed him. He is buried in Union Cemetery in Bakersfield, California.

Sarah was widowed in 1915, when John Kirk died of pneumonia at the age of seventy-nine. After her husband's death, she sold the farm to Daniel Doyle, listed her livestock and furniture for sale, and headed to California, escorted by her son Joseph. Sarah's son Richard was already living in California by this time.

We are sorry to have to report this week the death of Mr. John Kirk which occurred at his home on Wednesday of last week at the age of 75 years. Mr. Kirk has lived on the Island for thirty-five years, and had made many friends. He was a member of the Free Methodist Church and was faithful to the end. He has been failing in health for some time, but only a week previous to his death was he confined to his bed when he was stricken with pneumonia. During his illness he was very patient and trustful. He was a loving husband and father and a faithful friend. His was a happy cheerful disposition, and besides his immediate family he will be missed by a circle of friends. He was married to Miss Sarah Brown 34 years ago, and to this union was born four sons, three of whom are still living, Lex and Emerson of California, and Joseph at home, also a loving wife, who are left to mourn his loss, besides a host of friends. The funeral, which was held last Friday, and was conducted by Rev. Mr. Bailey, was largely attended.—Herald.

Death of John George Kirk, 1915. Sault Star, January 7, 1915.

Sarah arrived in Taft, California in December of 1915 with $2,000 in her pocket. That is the equivalent of about $60,000 in today's money. This allowed her to purchase her own home which was located near her son. It was a far cry from the desperate circumstances that her female relatives in Scotland faced upon the death of their husbands; this was a tribute to the changing times, and the opportunities that the New World presented.

FOR SALE—ONE MILCH COW, ONE mare, harness, rigs, cutter robes, furniture, range stove, box stove. Owner leaving. Nine months' credit given. Joseph Kirk, Richard's Landing P.O., St. Joseph Island.   213-5t-z

Sarah Brown Kirk. Notice of sale, 1915. Sault Star, 1915.

Between 1915 and 1929, Sarah endured the loss of her husband, step grandson, stepson, step daughter-in-law, and sons Alex and Richard. This was six family members now gone from her life—most while she was living in California, a world away from her siblings and close relatives.

Sarah continued to face these challenges and, after twenty-one years in California, on August 16, 1936, she passed away at the age of seventy-eight due to complications from a broken hip. She was laid to rest in West Side District Cemetery in Taft, Kern County, California, marking the end of a life filled with both resilience and heartache.

Resident of Taft Dies From Injury

TAFT, Aug. 18.—Mrs. Sarah Kirk, aged 78 years and a native of Scotland, died Sunday at the Taft Community Hospital, following complications that developed out of a broken hip received in an accident last week.

A mother of four children, she is survived by a son, Joseph Kirk of Taft and two sisters and a brother in the east.

Funeral services were held at the Taft Mausoleum Tuesday morning at 10 o'clock. The Nazarene Church will be in charge.

She has been a resident of Taft since 1915.

Obituary, Sarah Brown Kirk, 1936.

John Brown (1859–1932)
Gracious Integrity

John Brown.

John Brown and Janet Granger's eldest son John arrived on St. Joseph Island with his father, brother, and sisters in November 1878 when he was about nineteen years old. They immediately applied for their land and began to clear it. In the meantime, John; his father; and his brother, Sandy, stayed with their sister Mary Fisher and then with their sister Sarah Kirk.

To fulfill the requirements of the Homestead Act of 1868, John Sr. and his son John Jr. needed to clear forty-five acres of land and to build three dwellings. Initially, all the underbrush would have to be cleared and then the work of removing the trees would begin. Slashing was a common approach: trees were chopped down, left where they fell to dry out, and then later burned or taken out by horses or oxen to the sawmill. That was a job usually done in late fall or early winter, as it was much easier to haul the trees out when there was some snow on the ground.

Many hands make light work when it comes to tasks of this magnitude. Often a "logging bee" took place with neighbours arriving from near and far with equipment and teams to help get the job done. At the end of a long day, there was plenty of food, music, and dancing—sometimes well into the night to celebrate the event.

Men worked hard. Women worked miracles.[78]

Stumping, or removing the stumps from land that had been logged, was extremely difficult work. To get ahead on the cultivating requirement, turnips were often planted between the stumps. As well as working to clear their own property, the Brown men would also step in to help their neighbours.

By 1883, they had fulfilled all the settlement requirements and John Brown Sr. received a patent for his land consisting of Lots 9 and 10, Concession M. John Jr. received his patent for Lot 8, Concession M. These lots were in the centre of the Island in the area known as "The Mountain."

The original camp.

Lot 9, granted to John Brown Sr. in 1883, remains in the Brown family to this day. Initially used to pasture cattle, it has been used in more recent years for hunting and maple syrup production and it is often referred to as "the camp." This is a common term in Northern Ontario as it usually refers to a property that is rustic—one without amenities and that is used for shelter while logging and hunting.

Spring 2021. West Side Maple—Lot 9, Concession M, St. Joseph Island. Original property granted to John Brown in 1883.

Just prior to receiving his land patent in 1883, John Jr. married Prudence Boyce Shipman. Prudence was the daughter of Jehoiada Bryce Boyce Shipman and Jessie Dayson Davidson Irving. The Shipman (previously known as Shipton) family had come from England and had been in Connecticut since the mid-1600s. In the 1700s, Jehoiada's great-grandfather had settled in Upper Canada; he is a well-recognized United Empire Loyalist. John and Prudence initially took up residence on Lot 8, Concession M. In 1888, John Jr. purchased Lot 8, Concession L, just across the road and next door to his sister Sarah and her husband John Kirk. He continued to own Lot 8, Concession M, his original property, right up until his death.

John and Prudence had five children. Their eldest son, John "Jack" was born on May 29, 1882. At the age of twenty-nine in 1911, he was living on his own, farming, next door to his parents on St. Joseph Island. In the early 1920s, he was working in Grand Rapids, Michigan as a labourer for Golden and Boter Transfer Company.

He married Lillian Lucy Sanderson, and the couple had two children, Margaret "Lillie" and William John Brown. Jack's wife Lillian had previously been married to Frederick McLelland Aiken. Over the course of her life, she had thirteen children, and the paternity of some is unknown. On August 7, 1926, Jack was crushed by a steam shovel and he succumbed to his injuries. He was forty-four years old. He is buried in Fairplains Cemetery in Grand Rapids, Michigan.

BIG STEAM SHOVEL CRUSHES OUT LIFE

John Brown Receives Fatal Injury in Luce Plant Excavation.

John Brown, 44, employed by the Golden & Boter Transfer Co., was killed late Saturday when crushed in an excavation at the Luce Furniture Co. plant, Godfrey-av., by a steam shovel. He died a few moments after being rushed to St. Mary's hospital.

Brown was shoveling in the trench when the heavy swinging shovel struck him and wedged him against a wall. Coroner H. C. Wolfe ascribed death to internal hemorrhages.

Brown is survived by his widow, a son and a daughter residing at 443 Hastings-st., N. E. The body was taken to the A. B. O'Brien mortuary.

Grand Rapids Herald, August 8, 1926.

Lillian Lucy Sanderson Aiken Brown.

John Brown and Prudence Shipman's daughters Jessie and Margaret were born in 1885 and 1888, respectively. They married brothers Arken and Fay Eddy. After these daughters, John and Prudence had another daughter, Olive. Sadly, in November 1897, she passed away at just six months of age. In that year, from July to December, there were seven deaths registered on St. Joseph Island, four of which were children. Due to lack of medical care and medicines, one in five infants did not survive to their first birthday in those days. But Olive was not just a statistic, she was loved by her family, and she left a hole in their hearts as they grieved for her.

Olive Brown. Daughter of John Brown and Prudence Shipman. 1897.[79]

In 1906, about twenty-three years after the birth of their first child, son Lawrence was born. He married Mary Helen Hyland in 1938.

John and Prudence were members of the Mountain Church, where John was charged with serving communion. He always participated in the annual fall fair, and he won several prizes for a variety of entries—the most interesting being roses and whole wheat bread. His butter was also a regular winner over the years.

To market.[80]

John was a regular vendor at the farmer's market in Sault Ste. Marie. In the early years he made the trip by sailboat to the market. In later years good roads and ferry service made it possible to travel with his team of horses and a heavy wagon. The market was held Tuesdays from 9 am to 11 am. John would leave home on Monday, arriving in the Sault just before night-fall. Once the market had closed, John would make the journey home, arriving again just before dusk on Tuesday evening.

Butter and eggs were his mainstay along with apples, when in season. He developed a steady clientele and had a good reputation for quality products and for his honesty. His son Lawrence often made the trip with him. A quiet, shy boy, Lawrence observed his father's interaction with his customers from a distance. This would hold him in good stead in the future.

On March 8, 1932, John finished his morning chores, but upon returning to the house told Prudence that he wasn't feeling well. By late afternoon it was obvious he was in distress, and Prudence went to the barn to fetch Lawrence. By the time she returned to the house, John was taking his last breath. He was seventy-two years old.

His funeral was held at their home and conducted by Reverend William Howey and Reverend N. McQuarrie. Rev. Howey read from 2 Timothy 4:7 (RSV). "I have fought the good fight, I have finished the race, I have kept the faith." John was buried in the St. Joseph Township Cemetery.

John Brown. St. Joseph Township Cemetery.

He had indeed fought a good fight. He fulfilled the dream that his father had had for his family when they left their homeland to settle in Canada sixty-eight years before. Owning his own land, contributing to his community, and raising a hardworking successful family, he had finished his course.

Lawrence, now a young man, continued to run the family farm. He also carried on the tradition of being a market vendor, just like his father. Having watched his father over the years, he knew what it took to make a good deal and was fair to everyone. Just like his father, he had the gracious integrity of a good marketer who was respected by all.

After John's death, Prudence went to live with her daughter Jessie and she continued to live an active life. She suffered a stroke at age eighty-three and passed away on July 27, 1949; she is buried alongside her husband, John.

Jessie Alvina Brown Eddy and Prudence Shipman Brown.

Wedding of Lawrence Brown and Helen Hyland (left to right)
Oswald Shipman, Lawrence Alvin Brown, Helen Hyland, Vera Hyland
and Reverend John Hyndman wedding day, 1938.

Back standing (left to right) Arken Eddy, Clarence Eddy, Fay Eddy.
Middle row seated (left to right) John Brown, Jessie Brown, Margaret
Brown, Prudence Shipman. Front row (left to right) Russell Eddy,
Alvin Eddy, Ellen Eddy, Frederick Eddy, Alfred Eddy.

Alexander "Sandy" Brown (1862–1937)
Weathering the Great Depression

Alexander "Sandy" Brown.

lexander "Sandy" Brown was the youngest son of John Brown and Janet Granger. He was born when the family was living at Burnhead, Avondale, Scotland. Numerous family trees have assigned the name Kenneth as his middle name, but there has never been any official confirmation of that. Instead, "Sandy" was the informal name that stuck and that he was always called by.

Sandy was just two years old when the Brown family made the journey from Scotland to their first home in Canada:

Nissouri West Township in Middlesex County, Ontario. He attended school along with his brother John and sister Sarah and he helped on the farm as he grew older.

At sixteen years of age, and after the death of his mother, Sandy left southern Ontario with his father, his brother, and two of his sisters and relocated to St. Joseph Island. He worked alongside his father and brother to clear land and to establish their home. Their neighbours became his sister Sarah and husband John George Kirk and the John and Elizabeth (Mansfield) Wood family, whose eldest daughter, Isabella, would one day become his wife and the mother to their eight children.

Sandy Brown (1862–1937) and Isabella Wood (1876–1966).

Being very community-minded, Sandy was one of a group of men (which included his brother-in-law John Kirk) who made up the board of trustees for the first ever Mountain School. He also served for a time as a councillor for Jocelyn Township, the largest municipality on St. Joseph Island, and he was actively involved with his church.

Sandy farmed nearly until his death in 1937, raising animals as well as growing grain. All the hard work was worth it, and this was especially clear in the years of the Great Depression. Sandy's farm, along with the others on St. Joseph Island, became a source of sustenance for residents during these challenging times.

Although times were lean, the island's communities exhibited resilience by making do with the resources at their disposal. Being able to raise their own food was a great advantage to Sandy and his family. If one had to purchase food items from a store during that time, a pot roast was nine cents per pound, butter was ninety-five cents per pound, and picnic ham came in at seven cents per pound. But, at that time, the average net income for a farmer was only around $270 per year. Being able to harvest your own food had definite advantages.

Fast forward to today, and the same items now command significantly higher prices: pot roast is at seven dollars per pound, butter is at six dollars per pound, and a picnic ham is at five dollars per pound. However, while today's prices might seem steep, today's farmers have an average net income of about $134,000 per year.

Despite the profound impact that these dark years had on many Canadians (and particularly hard hit were the farmers in Western Canada), the residents of St. Joseph Island experienced a relatively milder effect. The scarcity of cash was a common challenge, but unlike their counterparts in the west, St. Joe farmers like Sandy found that their crops were not severely affected by drought and insect infestation as in the west.

In 1933, when national unemployment rates soared to 30 percent, the farmers on St. Joseph Island faced a shortage of off-season work opportunities, and thus a shortage of cash. In response, neighbours engaged in a barter system, exchanging goods like maple syrup for sugar or tea.

The ethos of the time was characterized by a collective effort to reuse, renew, or simply do without, as purchasing new items became a luxury few could afford. The resourcefulness and mutual support within the community underscored their ability to weather the economic challenges of the era.

Even amidst these uncertain times, almost all of Sandy and Isabella's children embarked on their own journeys—marrying and establishing homes of their own.

As his years advanced, Sandy's health began to decline. In his last years, he had gall bladder surgeries, including a very complicated and dangerous operation performed by Dr. Trefry. He also had several bouts of pneumonia and bronchitis. Sandy died at home on May 12, 1937, at the age of seventy-four. He is buried in the Mountain Maple Grove Cemetery on St. Joseph Island.

Having arrived in Canada at the age of two, he had followed in his father's footsteps, and he had worked tirelessly throughout his life achieving remarkable success. Seizing every opportunity that came his way, he left behind a legacy of hard work, resilience, and accomplishment. The story of Alexander "Sandy" Brown stands as a testament to the indomitable spirit of those who built their lives in the face of challenges and uncertainties.

***

John Brown and Janet Granger's family had arrived in Canada with a dream and few other possessions. The sheer determination and resilience of their generation is awe-inspiring. They left their homeland in Scotland and embarked on a journey to Canada where they were able to start anew and build a better life. It is truly remarkable to consider how they overcame the obstacles that they faced to achieve their dreams.

Their story is a testament to the opportunities and possibilities that Canada offered to newcomers during the nineteenth century as well as to the resilience and fortitude of those who were willing to take a chance to start again in a new land. Despite the hardships and tragedies that they faced, the Brown family was able to create a legacy that has lasted for generations, and it contributed to the fabric of the Canadian society that we all enjoy today.

Their story serves as an inspiration to all of us—reminding us of the power of hope, perseverance, and the human spirit.

It is interesting to note the longevity of the Brown women in this generation. Daughters Marion, Ellen, Mary, and Sarah all lived into their eighties. Perhaps there is something to be said about hard work and a simple farm life. Unfortunately, all these women married men who were considerably older than themselves, and they became widows at relatively young ages. Mary, for example, lived thirty-six years after her husband's death.

Thankfully, their families supported and cared for each of them after they became widows—exemplifying the unity of the Browns.

Part V

Inherited Journeys: The Next Generation of Canadians
Tursan air an sealbhachadh: An ath ghinealach de Chanèidianaich

The Family of Alexander "Sandy" Brown and Isabella Wood

Alexander "Sandy" (1862–1937) and Isabella (1876–1966)
Raising Their Family on Sandy Brown's Hill

In 1883, at age twenty-one, Alexander "Sandy" Brown purchased one hundred acres from Charles McArthur, who just months before had been awarded the property through a crown grant after he had completed the settlement requirements. Sandy purchased the property, Lot 11, Concession M, for $500. He now owned the adjacent property to his father John (1818–1901), who was awarded Lot 9 and Lot 10, Concession M that same year.

It would be seventeen years before Sandy would start to build the home that still stands on this property today. Until he got married, he lived with his brother John and sister-in-law Prudence. Imagine, Sandy was just twenty-one years old and yet he was the owner of one hundred acres of land! When his father had been that age, he had been a farm labourer in Scotland with no chance of ever owning land. Canada had indeed become the land of opportunity.

On December 30, 1898, at age thirty-six, Sandy married the girl next door, twenty-two-year-old Isabella Ann Wood. She was a first-generation Canadian; the family of her father (John Wood) had arrived on St. Joseph Island the same year that the Browns had. Additionally, both families had lived in Middlesex County near London before arriving on the island.

Isabella's father was originally from Doncaster, England and he had made it to Canada around 1866. He had married Elizabeth Ann Mansfield in 1875. At the time of his marriage to Elizabeth, John was already a widower. He was employed by the Darvill Stove Foundry in London, Ontario and returned there to work after being awarded his land grant on St. Joseph Island.

The income that he earned there would tide the family over during the lean times and would help pay for clearing his land. His daughter Isabella, (my great-grandmother) recalled that often there was not enough food to eat, and that they had often resorted to making hard tack from flour, water, and salt.

By 1901, Sandy and Isabella had two rooms to live in at the Lot 11, Concession M house that Sandy had started construction on the year before. It is more than likely that these two rooms were in the basement portion of the home. This house, with its two-foot-thick stone walls, would have been like a castle in comparison to the tenant cottages that the ancestral Browns had lived in in their native Scotland.

By 1921, there were seven livable rooms in the couple's home, as noted in the census; there were also two barns and outbuildings. Sandy had cleared timber and planted fruit trees and grain; he now had a sizable garden, some sheep and chickens, and a few cows and pigs.

Lot 11, Concession M, which many years later would come to be known as Poverty Hill or Sandy Brown's Hill, was where Sandy and Isabella had all their children. Between 1898 and

1911, they had two sons—John Duncan, known as Dunc, and Launcelot Alexander, known as Launce—and four daughters, Mary, Hazel, Gladys, and Sarah. They were surrounded by family, with their aunts and uncles and six cousins living nearby.

Home on Poverty Hill ink drawing. H. Phillips. 1975.

During the early to mid 1900s, as Sandy and Isabella's six children were growing up, there were several cases of smallpox on St. Joseph Island—and it even caused some deaths. The disease was sometimes called the speckled monster. A vaccine was available at the time, but many public health agencies did not promote or enforce it.

Thankfully, the Browns did not fall ill—though some of their neighbours did. Families were forced to quarantine in their homes and a placard was placed on the door warning of the infection. One of the Jocelyn Township councillors even suggested that, if anyone contracted the disease, their home and the contents of their home should be burned.

There was an outcry from residents saying that such a suggestion was outrageous. However, in 1903, Jocelyn Council awarded two families fifteen dollars to put toward the construction of new homes—provided that their existing homes were burned, along with any contents that could not be disinfected.

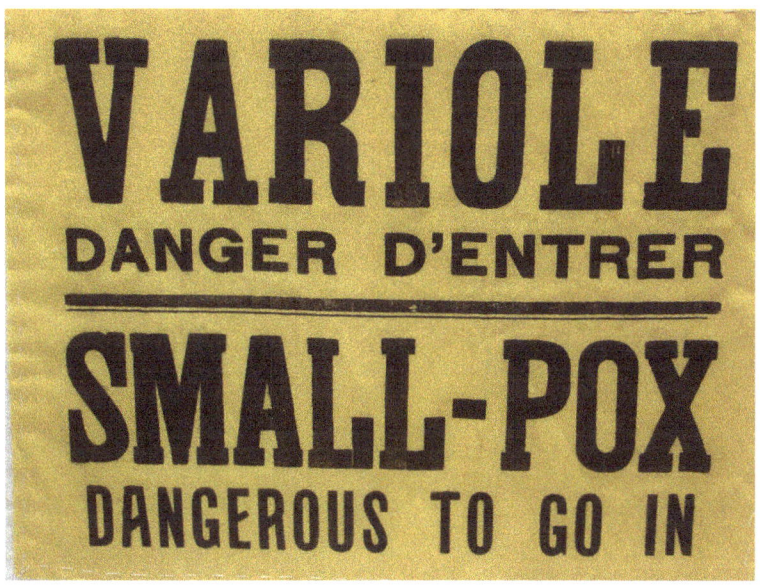

Small Pox warning banner – 1920-1930s.[81]

In mid-October 1914, Sandy and Isabella welcomed their seventh child, a daughter named Emily Pearl—affectionately known as Bessie. Her arrival, attended by Dr. Blackwell at their home, marked a moment of joy for the family. Tragically, Bessie's life was cut short at just fourteen months, as she succumbed to whooping cough in December of 1915. The family's grief was compounded when in the same month and year that Bessie died, Isabella had a stillborn baby whom they named William.

Facing the loss of two beloved infants at the same time must have been unimaginably devastating and heart-wrenching for Sandy and Isabella. This tragedy undoubtedly left an indelible mark on their lives and it reverberated throughout the entire family.

During this era, such heartbreak was regrettably common given the high rates of infant and child mortality in Canada—particularly in rural communities. The lack of accessible medical care and limited medicines led families to rely on home remedies passed down through generations.

For respiratory ailments, for example, the use of poultices made from a mixture of goose grease and camphorated oil or mustard was a prevalent practice to alleviate congestion.

The remaining Brown children, when not helping on the farm, attended a one-room schoolhouse—the Mountain School—which was about a three-kilometer walk from home. There were no school buses, and in winter the roads were not plowed—but that was no excuse for missing school or arriving late. Highlights for the children were the Christmas concert and the annual fall fair—highly anticipated events. The Brown children were regular participants, showcasing their talents or revelling in the community spirit—weaving memories that would last a lifetime.

Jocelyn S.S. No 2 or The Mountain School (1894–1952) where
the Brown children attended. In 1994, the Mountain School was
moved to the current location at the St. Joseph Township Centennial
Grounds and restored.

The boys also enjoyed hunting and fishing, and the entire
family took part in picnics, dances, and spirited card games.
Although the Browns could not afford one, visiting neighbours
with a gramophone or radio transformed ordinary evenings
into magical moments.

In 1930, due to his failing health, my maternal great-grandfather Sandy sold the family farm, Lot 11, Concession M, after
having owned it for forty-seven years! The purchaser was my

paternal great-grandfather Clarence Adelbert "Del" Haight. The sale price was $1,500 with a payment of $100 upon the signing of the agreement. The balance of $1,400 was to be paid in annual instalments of $100 plus interest over the next fourteen years. In 1935, when Del's son Walter married Sarah Delena Winnifred Smith, Del and his wife Jessie moved to another farm, this one along the Hilton Road—a major road on St. Joseph Island. (This second farm is now the site of All Tribes Christian Camp.) Walter and Sarah moved onto the farm on Lot 11, Concession M. They lived there for about twenty-two years and raised their four children there—including my father.

After the sale of the farm to Del Haight, Sandy and Isabella rented the Gilroy Farm on the C Line. With his health continuing to decline, Sandy sold off the remainder of his livestock and equipment in 1936, and the couple moved to a small farm in Richards Landing. This was located on the corner of Lucy Street and Elizabeth Street.

AUCTION SALE

Of farm stock, implements and furniture, will be held at the farm of Sandy Brown, Gilroy Estate, mile west of Richards' Landing, Ont., on Tuesday, April 28th, 1936, at one o'clock sharp as follows:

1 mare 11 years, 1 mare 5 years, 1 mare in foal 5 years, 1 cow seven years, milking, 1 cow 7 years, with calf at foot, 1 cow 6 years, due April 29, 1 cow 6 years, farrow, 1 cow four years, due April 23, 1 heifer 3 years, 1 heifer 2 years, 1 steer 1 year, hens, 1 Bain wagon, 1 Bain sleigh, 4 ft., 1 Massey-Harris mowing machine, 5 ft., 1 horse rake 9 ft., 1 Quebec riding plow, 1 finishing harrow, 1 turnip pulper, 1 Massey Harris discs, Outthrow, 1 hay rack, 1 hayrope and blocks, 1 buggy pole, 1 platform scales, 2,000 lbs. 1 cutter, 1 set double harness, whiffletrees, neckyokes chains, skidding tongs, 1 churn, 1 cream can, 8 gal. 1 heater, 1 cream separator, DeLaval No. 16, 1 dining room table and 5 chairs, 1 iron bed and springs. Other articles too numerous to mention.

Terms: All sums of $10 and under cash, over that amount 9 months credit on furnishing approved joint notes. Straight 5% off for cash.

SANDY BROWN, HARRY YATES, Prop. Auctioneer.

Alexander "Sandy" Brown's auction sale April 1936.

Although Sandy continued to farm on a smaller scale until 1936, his health would not allow him to do more. The following year, Alexander "Sandy" Brown passed away.

Isabella continued to live on the farm in Richards Landing for several years. She died in 1966 at the age of ninety and is buried in the Mountain Maple Grove Cemetery alongside Sandy.

In 1966 when Isabella died, her son John Duncan Brown purchased this headstone to commemorate her, his father, and two of his siblings.

As part of the second generation of immigrants to Canada, Sandy and Isabella passed on to their children the under-standing of the benefits of being able to own their own land and of the importance of being self-sufficient. In turn, their children passed this knowledge on to the fourth generation.

John Duncan "Dunc" Brown (1898–1975)
A Message For Future Generations

John Duncan Brown.

D unc, as he was affectionately known by family and friends, was the eldest child of Alexander "Sandy" Brown and Isabella Wood. He was born on April 30, 1898. As he was the eldest, and the only boy in the family for ten years, he worked alongside his father Sandy on the farm and he had his own chores of milking cows, feeding livestock, and bringing in firewood.

Many of these chores had to be completed in the morning before Dunc made his way to school, and they were repeated when he returned from his studies at the end of the day.

In the early spring, Dunc and his father would begin tapping trees, collecting sap, and boiling it down to make maple syrup. There is a long history of maple syrup production on St. Joseph Island, starting with the First Nation (Anishinaabe) population. Known then as ninaatigwaaboo (maple tree water), the process has been passed down through the generations.

St. Joseph Island is the largest producer of maple syrup in Ontario, and Dunc won many prizes at the agricultural fair for the quality of his maple syrup.

Gathering the sap.[82]

Doug Brown carrying on the tradition of maple syrup making just like his great-grandfather Sandy Brown and grandfather Dunc Brown.

Dunc lived his entire life on St. Joseph Island, except for his last few months. For most of his life he farmed, but he occasionally did some contract work for the township and some logging in Northern Ontario.

In 1925 he married Blanche Emily Cooper; they had three children—Lloyd Duncan, Harold James, and Emily "Betty" Elizabeth. A fourth child, a daughter, did not survive beyond her first couple of months.

Times were tough when Dunc and Blanche were raising their family. In the 1920s and 30s, men took work wherever they could find it. In 1928, the wheat harvest was beyond previous years so Dunc travelled out west to Saskatchewan because farm labourers were in high demand.

In the October 10, 1928, edition of the Montreal Gazette, it was reported that the grain crops of the three prairie provinces would be approximately one billion bushels—the largest yield since the start of the century. Just two years later, prairie farms would be devastated by drought, insect infestation, and the harsh impact of the Great Depression.

Before the introduction of the combine, prairie harvests would require large numbers of labourers for short periods of time. Harvest excursion trains brought workers west. Railways offered harvest tickets from any station (even as far away as the Maritimes) to Winnipeg for fifteen dollars, with a return fare being twenty dollars.

The accommodations onboard were crude. With four people packed per compartment, passengers slept on slatted wooden seats. Delays, crowding, and, on occasion, drunkenness led to riots. In the 1920s, railways demanded—and got—RCMP detachments who were placed on the trains to help keep order.

Harvest Train arriving in Western Canada.[83]

The harvesting work that Dunc did paid board and $1.75 to $2.25 for a ten-to-twelve-hour shift. The work usually lasted about fifteen days. A threshing crew of perhaps two dozen was paid $2.00 to $4.25 per person each day with board. Although the journey was rough and the work gruelling, these excursions introduced Canadians like Dunc to the Prairies. The work provided much needed funds which helped keep families going through the winter months.

Saskatchewan grain harvest.[84]

My grandfather Dunc was a man of few words, but I recall something that he said a long time ago that stuck with me. He commented that the next generations would probably not survive the hardships that he and the previous generations had experienced. No doubt he was right.

It's possible that Dunc thought that his grandchildren were spoiled, but it's also possible that he simply recognized the challenges that future generations would face in a rapidly changing world. Living through two world wars and the Great Depression would have given him a unique perspective on the potential hardships that future generations might face.

It's also possible that he wanted his grandchildren to be aware of the challenges that might lie ahead, and to be prepared to face them with the same resilience and determination that his generation had had when facing theirs.

Dunc died on December 4, 1975, and he is buried in the St. Joseph Township Cemetery.

Dunc's gravesite in St. Joseph Township Cemetery.

Mary Brown (1900–1955)
The Sault

Mary Brown.

Mary, the second child of Sandy and Isabella, was one of eleven babies born on St. Joseph Island during the second half of 1900. She attended the Mountain School along with her brother Dunc and her cousins, the Kirks and the Browns.

During her teen years, Mary occasionally took the steamer from Hilton Beach to the Sault to visit friends and relatives or to attend parties and other social events. When not helping at home, she led a busy social life with her friends Grace See and Ada Crowder. One such get together on the Island was a send-off for the local boys who were home on furlough from the fighting during the First World War.

In 1920, Mary had a daughter, Ruth Louise. Mary and Ruth lived at the home on the Mountain with Sandy and Isabella for the first two years of Ruth's life. After Mary's marriage and her move to Sault Ste. Marie, Ruth remained with Sandy and Isabella.

In June 1922, Mary wed William Clifton Snider, known as Cliff, in the manse of St. Paul's Presbyterian Church in Sault Ste. Marie. Cliff had been born in Teeswater, Ontario and had relocated to Thessalon, Ontario which is not far from St. Joseph Island. At the time of their marriage, Cliff was noted as a sailor.

Sault Ste. Marie, or as the locals affectionately call it "The Soo" was, and still is, the largest city in the Algoma District of Ontario.

Algoma Steel and the Abitibi Power and Paper Company both played a significant role in providing employment opportunities during this time. These opportunities attracted many immigrants to the area—primarily from southern Italy which included the Calabria region.

However, starting from the early 1920s to about 1929—when Mary and Cliff were raising their family—an unsettling and unpleasant presence began to emerge—the Ku Klux Klan.

While we often associate the Klan with the southern United States, it surprisingly established a chapter in Sault Ste. Marie with about six hundred members. They focused their vitriol and ire on the Italian Catholic population. Despite describing themselves as a social group, they excluded Catholics, immigrants, and black people from membership.

On several occasions disturbing events unfolded near Our Lady of Mount Carmel Catholic Church. This was just a short walk from the home of Cliff, Mary, and their children. Nighttime Klan gatherings and cross burnings took place—causing fear over the city and the neighbourhood.

Just imagine how horrifying that must have been for Mary and Cliff, knowing that this was happening right down the street. It was an eerie parallel to Mary's great aunt who had endured the Glasgow riots over seventy-five years earlier.

Although Mary lived about an hour's drive from her parents and sisters, she visited frequently—keeping their close-knit family bonded together. By 1935, Mary and Cliff had six children: William, Dorothy, Joyce, Erla, Helen, and Wayne. Cliff was driving a truck for a produce company, and he and his family were now living on Wilson Street in Sault Ste. Marie.

On February 21, 1936, Mary and Cliff welcomed their seventh child, a baby girl, Shirley Ann. Just ten days later, Shirley Ann died of dysentery. This devasted the family. Gladys, Mary's sister, came to stay for three weeks to help with the children and to console and provide support for Mary and her family.

Eight days before Christmas in 1955, Mary passed away from complications due to diabetes. She was laid to rest at the Greenwood Cemetery in Sault Ste. Marie.

Hazel Brown (1903–1939)
Between the States and Canada

Hazel Brown.

At around eighteen years of age, Sandy and Isabella's third child, Hazel, left St. Joseph Island to follow her heart to Michigan to be with Douglas Allison. During their relationship, a son, Robert "Bobby" Douglas Brown, was born in Bay City, Michigan in 1926. Although Bobby was known throughout his life as Bobby Allison, his birth registration is noted with the surname Brown, as Hazel and Douglas were not married. Unfortunately, the relationship encountered some challenges. This prompted Hazel's decision to return home to her parents on St. Joseph Island, bringing young Bobby with her.

In 1933, Hazel married Bernie Gay. They moved to Michigan

for a time but returned to St. Joseph Island after the birth of their son James in 1934. Interestingly, James spent most of his life not knowing that he had been born in the United States.

When he retired and applied for his pension— much to his surprise—he was advised that he was not a Canadian citizen. Having worked and contributed his entire life in Canada, you can imagine how difficult it was—and the time and paperwork it took—to straighten out the mess! To complicate matters even further, his father Bernie had used the alias "John Austin White" on the birth registration.

Hazel's sons James Gay (Gibbs) and Bobby Allison (Brown).

This would not be the first time that Bernie would use this alias on official documents. James, assuming that his name was James Bernie Gay, discovered (much to his surprise) that he had been registered at birth as James Bernie White.

In 1935 and 1937, Hazel and Bernie had two daughters, Beverly and Nancy. These joyous events were followed by heartbreaking ones just two years later. The first happened when the family suffered a fire on their Hilton Road farm which resulted in the loss of their barn.

The next occurred three weeks later. It started with Hazel experiencing labour pains and being rushed to the hospital in Richards Landing by her brother-in-law, Glynn Rains. The following day, June 29, 1939, Hazel had a baby boy who did not survive.

The next day Hazel died from complications from the birth. She was only thirty-five years old. Bernie was noticeably absent at the time of Hazel's death, as it was once again her brother-in-law Glynn Rains who had brought Hazel to the hospital and who had provided the necessary information for the registration of her death.

Hazel was survived by her four children, Nancy aged two, Beverly four, James five, and Bobby twelve. Bernie left the children with their sixty-three-year-old grandmother Isabella who now had to support them both emotionally and financially. Bernie was an absentee father to his three children as well as to two other children from a previous marriage.

To help make ends meet for her newly expanded household, Isabella maintained a large garden, a cow, and some chickens;

these allowed her to grow food and to sell milk and eggs in order to raise money.

(Back left to right) Bobby Allison (Brown), Isabella Wood Brown. (Front left to right) Nancy Gay and Beverly Gay July 1940

Nancy and Beverly continued to live with their grandmother Isabella until they had finished school and were out on their own. Isabella struggled to raise the four children, but it was painfully obvious that their father/stepfather Bernie had no interest in raising them. When another Island family wanted to adopt James, Bernie agreed, and James was adopted and raised by the Gibbs family.

A few years after his mother's death, Hazel's son Bobby returned to live with his father Douglas Allison in Michigan. He enlisted in 1944 and spent years in the Merchant Marines in San Diego, California. Sadly, at the age of fifty-eight, he was struck by a hit-and-run driver and killed on March 7, 1986. He was buried in San Diego. His family in Michigan had not heard from him in many years; they were not aware of his tragic death.

Pedestrian Killed in Hit-Run Accident

LAKESIDE—A 58-year-old man was killed by a hit-and-run driver Friday night as he walked on Woodside Avenue near Winter Gardens Boulevard in Lakeside, the California Highway Patrol said.

Robert Allison of Lakeside was in the middle of the road when he was struck by a late-model pickup at about 7 p.m. He died three hours later at El Cajon Medical Center.

The hit-and-run vehicle is described as a white 1982 to 1984 Ford Ranger pickup with a camper shell and damage to the right front and right center of the truck's body. It also has a buckled hood, the CHP said.

Robert Allison death. Los Angeles Times. March 9, 1986.

We see from Hazel's life story that infant mortality and child-birth deaths in the early twentieth century were still crushing realities for families—including the Browns. But we also see that family members and people in the community often stepped in to fill the tremendous gaps that these tragedies left.

Gladys Margaret Brown (1905–1988)
An Award-Winning Baker

Gladys Margaret Brown.

S andy and Isabella's fourth child, Gladys Margaret, was born at home on The Mountain in 1905. Gladys attended the Mountain School and she was an honour student. She was very athletic and she also won several first-place awards for her pies and bread at the annual school fair.

She had a reputation throughout her life as an exceptional cook and she enjoyed crocheting, embroidery, and other crafts. Even in her senior years, her handiwork was displayed at various events. Over the years, many of us were gifted with her beautiful handmade treasures for birthdays, showers, and weddings.

In 1930, Gladys married her sister's brother-in-law, Ernest "Ernie" Snider, in the parsonage of Central United Church in

Sault Ste. Marie. For a while after their marriage, Gladys and Ernie lived with Gladys's parents, Sandy and Isabella.

Ernie worked on lake freighters and could be gone for prolonged periods of time. Sandy and Isabella were empty nesters by this time so I'm sure that they appreciated Gladys's company and Gladys would have enjoyed cooking meals and keeping busy while her husband was away.

Occasionally, during the summer months Gladys would accompany Ernie on one of the freighters. It was not uncommon for spouses to travel with their partners. While the living conditions were often basic, it allowed the couple to be together and it was an enjoyable change of scenery for Gladys.

One such trip for Gladys was in 1936 when she accompanied Ernie onboard The Waterton. This vessel was approximately 258 feet in length and it primarily transported iron ore and grain. The freighter was built in 1928 in England, went through many ownership changes, and in 1941 was pulled from its Great Lakes service to be sent to the Atlantic during the Second World War. In October 1942 it was torpedoed and sunk by a German submarine off Cape Breton Island.

During Gladys's trip in 1936 the morning routine would begin early—at around dawn. Breakfast was served in the ship's galley with Ernie and Gladys enjoying a hearty breakfast of eggs, bacon, and fresh bread. While Ernie was off working, Gladys would explore the freighter and spend time chatting with the crew or other spouses.

Throughout the day Gladys could read, write letters, work on her embroidery, and enjoy the scenery. Lunch might include sandwiches and soups while dinner might feature fresh caught fish. The evenings were a time for socializing where everyone would gather to play cards, share stories, and enjoy each other's company. On clear nights, Gladys and Ernie could stroll on deck to stargaze and to enjoy the tranquility of the open water and spectacular lake views.

Ernest and Gladys Snider. Mountain Maple Grove Cemetery, St. Joseph Island.

By the end of the Great Depression and the beginning of the Second World War, Gladys and Ernie had moved to Hearst Street in Sault Ste. Marie. Ernie's job was secure during this time, as lake freighters were kept busy transporting iron ore, coal, and other raw materials for the war effort.

Gladys and Ernie did not have any children of their own, but they often had their nieces visit for weekends and holidays. Gladys enjoyed teaching them how to bake, and to do crafts and needlework.

Ernie passed away in 1976 and Gladys in 1988. Both were laid to rest at the Mountain Maple Grove Cemetery on St. Joseph Island. A helper her entire life, Gladys was always willing to support her family and to care for others should the need arise.

Launcelot "Launce" Brown (1908–1929)
Tragedy at the Dock

Launcelot Alexander Brown. The story is told that the Remington rifle in this photo was manufactured around about 1917. Launce walked across the ice in the winter of 1928 to Michigan and purchased it. It is now proudly owned by Launce's great nephew Ryan Brown.

A tragic accident on July 21, 1929, would once again devastate the Brown family. Sandy and Isabella's twenty-one-year-old son Launce, his cousin Alvin Eddy, and his friend Gordon Gapp had all gathered at the P Line dock. Although Launce could not swim, for some unknown reason—perhaps simply to show off for his friends—he jumped off the dock into twelve feet of water. Alvin and Gordon realized immediately that Launce was in trouble, but their frantic attempts to rescue him were unsuccessful.

Gordon then ran to Fred Clark's for help. Fred had the nearest farm, but it was about two kilometers away. He was able to retrieve Launce's lifeless body and bring it to shore.

Launce's funeral was held the following day at home, with many families and friends in attendance. He was described as having a bright and kindly disposition and he was respected by all. Alvin Eddy and Gordon Gapp, who had bravely tried to save him, were among his pallbearers.

Launcelot Alexander Brown was buried in the Mountain Maple Grove Cemetery. The Brown family was shattered by this loss and extended their sincerest gratitude to those who had tried to rescue him. The loss of this young man took a tremendous toll on his father Sandy's already declining health.

The Browns' story here continues to reflect the harsh realities of the time and it underscores the resilience that was required to navigate the challenges of family life in an era marked by both joy and sorrow.

Sandy and Isabella's ability to carry on despite these profound losses speaks to the deep love and determination that bound this family together.

Launce Brown Drowns At St. Joe Island Dock

Jumped Into 12 Feet of Water at Noon Yesterday, Though Unable to Swim; Attempted Rescue by Gordon Gapp Failed; Body Recovered by Frank Clark

A regrettable drowning accident took place at the "P line" dock, St. Joe Island, at noon yesterday, when Launce Brown, aged 21, son of Mr. and Mrs. Alexander Brown of St. Joe, who was bathing at the place with Alvin Eddy, and Gordon Gapp lost his life.

The water is some 12 feet deep at the dock and Brown was unable to swim. Just before he entered the water he said that, although he could not swim, that "this is as good a time as any to learn." He then jumped into the water, and when he came to the surface it was seen by the others that he was in difficulty. Brown seemed to be stunned and helpless. It is now believed that the shock of the cold water affected him.

Young Gapp, himself a poor swimmer, made several attempts to rescue Brown from the water, but without success. When the body finally disappeared Gapp hurried to the farm of Frank Clark, a mile and a quarter distant, and Mr. Clark, hurrying to the dock, recovered the body and brought it ashore. The funeral will take place at Richards' Landing this afternoon at three o'clock.

In addition to his parents the victim of the accident leaves one brother, Duncan, and four sisters, Mrs. Clifford Snider, Trelawn Avenue, Soo, Mrs. Glynn Rains, St. Joe Island and Gladys and Hazel at home. He was a nephew of Mr. and Mrs. Charles Eddy, 403 Bruce street.

Drowning accident. Sault Daily Star, July 1929.

Family photo taken the day of Launce's funeral, July 22, 1929.
Front row (left to right) Joyce Snider, Ruth Brown, Dorothy Snider,
William Snider. Second row (left to right) Gladys Brown with baby
Erla Snider, Alexander (Sandy) Brown, Isabella Wood Brown,
Sarah Brown Rains, Mary Brown Snider. Back row (left to right)
William Clifton Snider, Glynn Rains.

Sarah Isabella Brown (1911–1993)
A Busy Social Life

Sarah Brown.

The youngest child of Sandy Brown and Isabella Wood, Sarah Isabella Brown was born at home in 1911. She attended the Mountain School, and like her sister Gladys, was an honour student. Sarah, as you may recall, is the one who provided me with the list of family members that started me on my long quest of building my Brown family tree.

In March 1929, just a few months prior to the untimely death of her brother Launce, Sarah married Glynn Harold Rains. She was seventeen years old. They made their home near the shore of the St. Marys River on St. Joseph Island at a place known as the Sailors Encampment.

The name Sailors Encampment dates to at least 1854 when ships—frozen in the ice due to the lateness of the season—had to spend the winter in the river. Glynn was the groundskeeper and overall handyman for Mrs. Margaret Hyatt, an American who owned tourist cottages (Milburn Cottage and Seagull Lodge) and her summer home at Journey's End. Thanks to his talents, Mrs. Hyatt's gardens were admired by all.

Wintery night.[85]

Sarah and Glynn were hardworking individuals with a vibrant social life. As active members of the Encampment Cribbage Club, they frequently hosted gatherings at their home. They also occasionally joined the Jolly Dozen Cribbage Club. Each game night saw twelve players competing for prizes, with a hearty lunch served around midnight. The spread typically included sandwiches—or slices of ham or roast beef or chicken—all accompanied by pickles, relishes, bread, and rolls. For dessert, there were pies, cakes, or cookies enjoyed with hot tea or coffee.

During the winter months, it wasn't uncommon for players to arrive by horse and sleigh when the roads were impassable. Sarah and Glynn's door was always open to visitors—whether nieces, nephews, Sarah's sisters, her mother, or their many friends. Everyone was welcome.

Marshmallow roasts on the shore, dances at Kentvale Hall, the fall fair, and Christmas concerts made for a very busy, fun-filled household.

Sarah and Glynn raised their four children, Orrell, Gordon, Clara Jean, and Roberta at this idyllic St. Joseph Island spot, all while being surrounded by their extended family. In the mid-1950s, now that all of their children were married and had lives of their own, Glynn and Sarah decided to move to Sault Ste. Marie where Glynn was working for the Abitibi Power and Paper Company. They purchased some property in the east end of Sault Ste. Marie (Manitou Park), and construction began on their new home in 1958.

In October of that year, Sarah's husband Glynn and their son-in-law Paul Nelson—the husband of Clara Jean—headed out in a small motorboat on a hunting trip. The following morning, their empty boat was discovered by the US Coast Guard. It had sunk in American waters off Burnt Island. The small dog that had accompanied them was found on nearby Butterfield Island, and a pair of oars and a gas can were subsequently found on nearby Drummond Island.

The US Coast Guard along with family and friends searched continuously for several days but to no avail. Finally, in mid-November, Glynn's remains were found on a small island not far from St. Joseph Island. This discovery renewed efforts to find Paul.

Almost two years later, in October of 1960, hunters found Paul's remains on a small Michigan island. It was such a tragic conclusion and an immense loss for the families of these two men.

Sadly, this meant that Sarah had to move by herself into the new home that she and Glynn had built. She began working as a nanny/housekeeper for the McKinney family on Borron Avenue—walking an hour there and back each day. She cooked, cleaned, and looked after the two little McKinney boys, becoming quite attached to and fond of this family.

In her spare time, she made beautiful quilts for the new babies in the family and for wedding gifts. She was a gifted seamstress, and she sewed dresses, skirts, and suits. Just like her husband Glynn, Sarah was a talented gardener; she surrounded her home with lovely gardens that were filled with Sweet Williams,

Foxglove groves, and different varieties of sunflowers. She developed a long and lasting friendship with her neighbour Mrs. Cudlip and remained an avid card player well into her senior years.

Sarah was always impeccably dressed, soft-spoken, gentle, very proper, and kind. She passed away at the age of eighty-one, leaving a legacy of four children, thirteen grandchildren, and twenty-three great-grandchildren.

***

Raising a family during the Great Depression and the Second World War presented numerous challenges to Sandy, Isabella, and their family. It required each of them to be resilient and adaptable. Although the losses of Launce, Mary, Hazel, and babies Bessie and William were devastating to the members of the family, they were always there for one another. They were unwavering in their support of each other whether it was during a tragic loss or a joyful celebration.

Sandy and Isabella's children and grandchildren always seemed to be drawn home for family celebrations that were filled with love and laughter and that created memories that would last a lifetime. It seems that they understood the hardships and difficulties that their parents and grandparents had endured, and—with that stoic Scottish determination—they continued to get on with it—making the best of what life had to offer.

Part VI

Settling into Community
Suidhich sa choimhearsnachd

The Family of John Duncan "Dunc" Brown
and Blanche Cooper

John Duncan "Dunc" (1898–1975) and Blanche Cooper (1897–1947) A Respected Family

A man of few words, Dunc exuded a quiet demeanor, a trait that was inherent in his Scottish heritage. He was mischievous, with a dry sense of humour, and this was coupled with a no-nonsense attitude and a touch of stubbornness that defined his character. He had a love of horses and owned several over the years. Dunc was often called upon for his amateur veterinary guidance should someone have had a sick or injured horse.

In 1920, he entered his team in harness in the fall agricultural fair in Richards Landing on St. Joseph Island. It is noted in the Sault Star that he won the drivers competition. Dunc also won the hauling contest, with his team pulling three thousand five hundred pounds of stone. I'm sure living up on the mountain gave him lots of practice in hauling stones. He placed second for his plums and first for his butter and maple sugar. He was an avid reader of western novels, and, in later years, he loved watching the hockey game on Saturday night.

On Tuesday, July 7, 1925, at four o'clock in the afternoon, John Duncan Brown married Blanche Emily Cooper at her parents' home, The Evergreens, in Harmony on St. Joseph Island. It was an outdoor affair, with the vows being exchanged on the verandah and guests seated on the lawn. Peonies, roses, and ferns decorated the verandah and tables, and Blanche wore orange blossoms in her hair.

Dunc and colt, Bonnie. D Line Farm, St. Joseph Island.

John Duncan Brown and Blanche Emily Cooper wedding. July 7, 1925.

Blanche was born in 1897, the daughter of Annie Mary Brown and Charles Francis Cooper. Blanche's maternal grandparents were Henry Joseph Brown and Emily Ann Boxall. They had emigrated from Kent, England to Canada in 1870, and they had settled in Middlesex County upon their arrival. The opportunity for land ownership had drawn them to St. Joseph Island around 1879—as it had done for so many others.

Blanche had three sisters and one brother, Marguerita "Reta," Helene, Edith, and Charles Arthur "Brown." Blanche, Reta and Helene all attended the North Bay Normal School, which nowadays would be called a teachers' college. After graduating around 1915, Blanche got her first teaching position at the Alma Heights School in Thessalon.

She then taught at the Mountain School from 1917 to 1920. In the winter months throughout this second teaching assignment, Blanche boarded with Dunc's parents, Sandy and Isabella. As Dunc was still living at home during this time, perhaps this was the start of their budding romance.

Blanche later taught at the Harmony School, C Line School, served as the secretary treasurer to the trustees there, and taught Sunday school. She taught piano as well—in the winter making her way on snowshoes to give lessons at various homes. Always well-liked by her students and well respected by the community, Blanche was also very involved with the women's institute and her church.

Henry Joseph Brown and Emily Ann Boxall, grandparents of Blanche
Emily Cooper.

Blanche Emily Cooper graduation. North Bay Normal School. 1915.

In 1926, Dunc and Blanche celebrated the arrival of their first child, a son, Lloyd Duncan. The family grew once more in 1930 with the birth of their second son, Harold James. It was fourteen months later, in December of 1931, that a daughter, Marguerite Adelaide, was born. She was diagnosed with spina bifida at birth, and Blanche's parents provided invaluable support, inviting Blanche and Marguerite to stay with them.

Two months later little Marguerite passed away; the family gathered for a somber funeral at The Evergreens to bid her farewell. She was laid to rest in the St. Joseph Township Cemetery, leaving behind a legacy of love and a heart-wrenching reminder of the challenges that life can sometimes present.

INFANT DAUGHTER OF MR. AND MRS. D. BROWN PASSES

Kentvale, Feb. 16.—The infant daughter of Mr. and Mrs. Duncan Brown passed away yesterday at the home of Mr. and Mrs. C. F. Cooper, Mrs. Brown's parents, where she has been staying the last two weeks. The baby has not been well for some time so death was not unexpected but the deep sympathy of the community and friends is extended to the bereaved parents. Rev. H. Howey conducted the funeral service at the home after which interment was made in the Landing cemetery.

Obituary of infant Marguerite Adelaide Brown. 1932.

In 1933, Dunc purchased a farm on the D Line on St. Joseph Island, and in May 1934 he moved his family there from the rented Gilroy farm. This property had originally been owned by Benjamin McIntyre through a land grant issued in 1884. In 1893 it had been sold to Elijah Good and in 1903 it had been purchased by James Harron.

In 1907 James Harron transferred the property to his son Charles Harron. Charles died in 1927, and Dunc purchased the farm from his estate for $2,000. He put $500 down and mortgaged the rest for twenty years from the Ontario, Agricultural Development Board. The documents list his collateral: four horses, twelve cows, nine sheep, one pig, two plows, a thirteen-disc seed drill, finishing harrows, a cultivator, a mower, a hay rake, a hay loader, a binder, a manure spreader, a wagon, a buggy, and a cream separator.

Dunc's father Sandy and mother Isabella moved into the Gilroy farm on the C Line that Dunc and family had just vacated. In August of 1934, not long after the purchase of the farm, Dunc and Blanche welcomed a daughter—my mother—Emily Elizabeth (Betty).

Blanche suffered from asthma, and living on the farm seemed to worsen her condition. For a few years during the winter months, husband Dunc and sons Lloyd and Harold had worked on the Algoma Central Railway (ACR) for a pulpwood company in Hansen, south of Hearst, Ontario. Blanche's doctor thought that Hansen had a better climate for her health and suggested that a move there would be beneficial.

To avoid having to transport children to Hearst so that they could go to school there, Northern Paper Mills had started their own school. In 1944, they placed an advertisement for a schoolteacher who would teach grades one through eight at an annual salary of $1200.

Blanche applied and secured a teaching contract. She and daughter Betty boarded the ACR in September 1944 and they made their way to Hansen in preparation for the school year.

WANTED—PUBLIC S C H O O I
teacher at Hansen, Ontario, District
of Algoma, for Grades 1-8. Salary
$1,200 basis. State age, qualifications
experience, with name of last, inspector. Duties to start January 3rd
Apply to Northern Paper Mills, Limited.   j208-6t

Advertisement for teacher. Sault Daily Star, 1944.

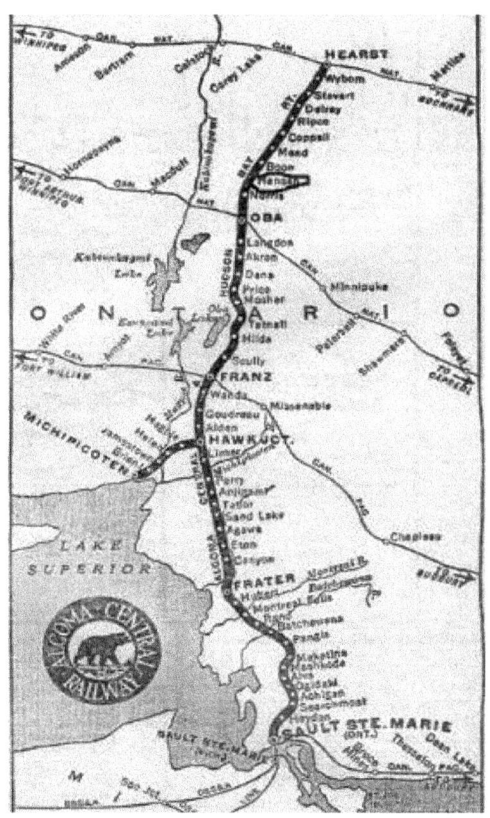

Algoma Central Railway line from Sault Ste. Marie to Hearst, Ontario.

Remains of the Northern Paper Mills camp, Hansen.

Northern Paper Mills camp school Hansen.

Unfortunately, Blanche was hospitalized on more than one occasion while in Hansen. She described her situation in letters written to her sister-in-law Sarah Brown Rains. These letters were later given to my mother, Betty, as treasured keepsakes.

In a letter dated June 1946, Blanche voiced her frustration:

> This Dr. seems to depend entirely on amoxicillin, and it simply poisons my stomach. I took the pills a week and then he had some dissolved in a fluid and injected by intravenous.

Blanche felt that if they didn't find another solution soon, she would be in hospital for the entire summer.

The final letter that Blanche wrote to her sister-in-law Sarah was written over a three-day period in March 1947. In it, she expressed her concern that she still needed to pay her Women's Institute membership; she was also thankful that her employer was continuing to pay her wages and her healthcare benefits. Universal healthcare was not legislated in Canada until 1957, so Blanche was grateful to have private coverage through her employer.

On August 6, 1947—a few months after writing this last letter— Blanche passed away at just fifty years of age. From the stories that I have heard about her throughout my life, I wish she had lived long enough for me to get to know her. These excerpts from her obituary express the loss that was felt by her family and by the community as a whole:

Obituary

Mrs. Duncan Brown St. Joseph Island was saddened to hear of the death of Mrs. Duncan Brown, which occurred at the Plummer Memorial Hospital, Sault, on August 6. The late Mrs. Brown was a member of one of the island's most respected families and she herself was held in the esteem of all who knew her for her never failing kindness, cheerfulness and willingness to do her share in the local public life. For the past eight years she had been a sufferer from chronic asthma, against which she battled bravely to the last. Much sympathy is felt for her husband, mother and family.

The funeral took place on Friday from the home of one of her sisters, Edith, to St. Mark's United Church, Richards Landing and was marked by a wonderful manifestation of sympathy and respect from a church packed with her sorrowing relatives and friends. Captain the Rev. Edgar Gill officiated and delivered a most comforting message of Christian hope and assurance.

Miss Ann Grexton presided at the organ, and the hymn "Abide with Me" was sung. Mr. Clyde Cumming sang as a solo, "The Old Rugged Cross". Pallbearers were Greydon, Clarence and Earl Kent, Cliff and Ernest Snider and Russel Campbell.

The church was decked with a magnificent display of floral tributes from many friends, including the Sailor's Encampment W.I., St. Marks W.A. and the Ladies' Auxiliary of the Canadian Legion. Interment was in Richards Landing Cemetery.

It was twenty-five years after his wife Blanche's death that Dunc married Elizabeth Mae Rains, widow of George Thomas Girard. Dunc moved from the D Line farm to Mae's home in Richards Landing.

John Duncan Brown and Mae Rains Girard. 1973.

Dunc passed away at the age of seventy-seven and is buried in the St. Joseph Township Cemetery.

John Duncan Brown. St. Joseph Township Cemetery, St. Joseph Island.

Lloyd Duncan Brown (1926–1975)
Enjoying Community Organizations

Lloyd Duncan Brown.

Lloyd, the eldest son of Dunc Brown and Blanche Cooper, was involved in many activities and organizations growing up. He was a member of the St. Joseph Island Drum and Trumpet Band, the Boy Scouts, I Line baseball team and the Junior Farmers. He attended many dances—often taxiing friends to them in the cutter or his car.

Lloyd enjoyed being involved in community events; he was very social, and he was always encouraging others to join in. In 1943 and 1944, he worked on board the MV Algosteel and the SS Royalton.

SS Royalton. In operation 1924-1979.[86]

As a member of the crew on these ships he would have been responsible for handling cargo and for regular maintenance tasks such as cleaning and maintaining the ship's deck, handling ropes, and ensuring that the ship was in tiptop shape. Life on these ships was often tough; the hours were long, and the conditions were challenging.

In 1944, he travelled twice to Manitoba to work in the grain harvest. Lloyd also spent a few winters in Hansen where he worked for Northern Paper Mills as a general labourer. He moved materials, cleaned, and maintained equipment. As an adult and family man, he worked in a sawmill, drove a transport truck, and spent many hours on the road.

Due to Blanche's illness, neither Dunc nor Blanche could attend Lloyd's marriage to Catherine Cain in July of 1947. When Blanche was in hospital just before she died, newlywed Catherine came to stay at the Brown farm. She helped with meals and other household tasks.

This would have been a busy time of year on the farm, and her help would have been greatly appreciated. Neighbours would have been working together to get the hay and grain off the fields. Catherine and the other women in the community would have been responsible for feeding the men. Teaming up, they would have prepared a huge meal at noon consisting of beef; chicken; ham; mashed potatoes; bread or biscuits; homemade butter and jam; and beans, peas, and tomatoes—all fresh from the garden. The meal would not have been complete without dessert—usually pie. Now well fed, the men would have returned to the fields or moved on to the next farm.

Loading hay.[87]

Lloyd and Catherine stayed for a time at the old Brown camp (the original John Brown (1818–1901) property) on the Hilton Road. As their family grew, they eventually moved to a larger accommodation at the corner of 10th Side Road and F & G Line Road on St. Joseph Island.

They then moved to Sault Ste. Marie with their five children where they lived on Goetz Street. In the early 1970s, they moved to Thunder Bay as Lloyd had a job opportunity there.

Lloyd suffered from asthma like his mother Blanche and he also had other health issues. He passed away in Thunder Bay on May 9, 1975 at the age of forty-eight. Catherine stayed in Thunder Bay until her death in September of 1989.

Harold James Brown (1930–2013)
Wearing Many Hats

Harold James Brown.

Dunc and Blanche's son Harold was always an active participant in the fall fairs. He often won first place for his poultry, produce, and flowers. Throughout his life, his garden was always meticulously kept, and you would have been hard-pressed to find even a single weed in his garden.

When he was about twelve years old, Harold was raking hay with the team when the horses were spooked by something. He fell from the rake and was trampled by the team. It took him some time in the hospital in Richards Landing to recover.

As a teen, Harold worked at the Kentvale store, and as an adult he was a school board trustee and a grader operator for the township. Like his father Dunc and brother, Lloyd, Harold also spent some winters in Hansen working for Northern Paper Mills.

Harold passed on his gardening skills to his children.
A sample of his son, Doug's, immaculate garden.

In 1961, he purchased two school buses and began transporting students to the Island schools and to the high school in Desbarats. All the while, he maintained his farm with some dairy cattle, chickens, sheep, and, as I recall, a very nasty banty rooster.

When he moved his family into Richards Landing, he also had a garage where he repaired everything from lawnmowers to cars. He coached baseball for many years, and in 1965, his team won their third consecutive championship—a testament to his leadership and commitment to his community.

In September of 1948, Harold married Coyla Belle Anderson. They, just like Lloyd and Catherine had, lived for a time at the old Brown camp on the Hilton Road. They then moved into the village of Hilton Beach, and in August of 1949, they moved to the D Line farm where they raised their three children.

1975 would mark the end of the Brown family farming legacy that had been started by Harold's great-grandfather John Brown (1818–1901) in the Parish of Avondale, Scotland. Harold and Coyla built a new home in the village of Richards Landing near the property where Harold's grandparents Sandy and Isabella had lived. Harold and Coyla lived there until 2012, when ill health forced them to leave their beloved home.

Harold passed away on July 7, 2013, and Coyla on August 20, 2014. Both have been laid to rest in the St. Joseph Township Cemetery.

Harold and Coyla Brown. St. Joseph Township Cemetery.

Emily Elizabeth "Betty" Brown (1934–2004)
A Big Heart

Emily Elizabeth "Betty" Brown.

B etty was only twelve years old in 1947 when her mother Blanche died. Dealing with his own grief—and having to keep the farm running—Dunc thought it best for Betty to stay for a time in Orillia with her Aunt Helene who was one of her mother's sisters. With money pinned to her undershirt, she was taken to the train station, and she made her way on her own.

Betty had never been separated from her family before and she was terrified about traveling alone. Once she reached her destination, she became very homesick. To keep her occupied, Helene gave Betty five cents each day to bicycle to the butcher shop to buy liver for her cat.

Emily Elizabeth "Betty" Brown with brother Harold James Brown. 1934.

I am uncertain how long my mother stayed in Orillia after her mother's death, but when reminiscing about that period in her life, she said that she was very homesick and that she missed her father and brothers and wanted desperately to return home.

Betty had a big heart and she always had a soft spot for animals. In April of 1947, the same year her mother passed away, she was returning from Hansen with her brother Lloyd when a situation arose that put her love for animals to the test. While crossing the ice to get to the Island, their car became stuck in the slush.

Betty had five pet rabbits and her cat with them on this trip. She was in tears and pleaded with her brother Lloyd as she refused to leave the animals behind in the car. Lloyd relented and they carried the animals the three kilometers across the ice to safety. This would not be the last time that Betty would speak up for animals.

Throughout her life, she rescued and cared for cats, dogs, rabbits, horses, and chickens, to name a few. She believed that they all deserved a safe and caring home.

In 1949, at age fifteen, Betty accepted a position with the housekeeping staff at the Mathews Memorial Hospital in Richards Landing. She remained there until her marriage in 1952. In August of that year, Betty married Wilfred George "Bill" Haight. They left St. Joseph Island and moved to a home on Woodcroft Avenue in Sault Ste. Marie.

In 1968, Betty and Bill purchased fifteen acres in Prince Township, just outside the Sault Ste. Marie city limits. They built a home and a barn which allowed them to keep horses, laying hens, and whatever stray or homeless animal that had shown up at their door.

Like her aunts Gladys and Sarah, Betty was a beautiful seamstress. She also knitted, crocheted, quilted, and made other handmade crafts.

Bill was a musician; this kept him busy on weekends along with his fulltime job as an aircraft firefighter. At the age of forty-five, Betty obtained her registered nursing assistant certificate and she worked for many years after in a long-term care facility.

In July of 2000, due in part to Betty's failing health, Bill and Betty sold their home in the Sault and returned to their roots on their beloved St. Joseph Island. Betty would pass away in August of 2004 and Bill just three short months later. They were both laid to rest at the St. Joseph Township Cemetery.

Bill and Betty Haight. St. Joseph Township Cemetery.

****

This generation of the Brown family experienced major shifts—not just in family dynamics—but also in the workforce and the economy. They sought full and part time work off the farm and, in some cases, moved to urban areas. Lloyd Brown left the Island, moved to Sault Ste. Marie, and then went on to Thunder Bay to pursue work opportunities. Harold continued to farm on a part time basis and he took on additional work within the community. Post war opportunities in the workforce allowed for dual income families. Much to her credit, Betty returned to school and subsequently pursued a career in healthcare.

> The history of our grandparents
> is remembered not with rose
> petals but in the laughter and
> tears of their children and their
> children's children. It is into us
> that the lives of the grandparents have gone.
> It is in us that their history becomes a future.
>
> —Charles and Ann Morse

Part VII

Thank You for Dreaming

Tapadh Leibh airson Bruadar

Dreaming of a Better Future

My maternal Browns—who had lived in the harsh conditions of Easdale Island and who had worked in the Island's unforgiving slate quarries—had needed to be of strong body and character. Those who chose to make their way to Glasgow during the Industrial Revolution had faced their own hard challenges—ones that became intermixed with tragic circumstances. Their pursuit of a brighter future was fraught with persistent struggles as they navigated the complexities of an era that was marked by profound societal and economic change.

Their attempt to carve out a better life for themselves in the wake of industrialization demanded resilience in the face of adversity and a tenacious spirit to overcome the formidable obstacles that defined their path.

It was not until fourteen years after leaving Scotland for Canada that John Brown (1818–1901) finally started the grueling process of becoming a landowner. At the age of sixty, when nowadays we are looking to retire, the hard work had only just begun for John and his sons.

There was plenty of timber to be cleared, homes to be built, land to be cultivated, crops to be grown, and pasture and livestock to be developed—all in an effort to live sustainably on their own land. Keep in mind that trying to cultivate land on "The Mountain" on St. Joe was not always easy. As the saying goes, "they grew potatoes and stones and in most years the latter was the better crop." With each generation, though, life improved. At least John Brown and his descendants didn't have to import soil for their gardens from Ireland!

The Brown family faced numerous challenges in their journey to Canada and in their efforts to build a new life in a new land. They experienced poverty, illness, and other hardships. However, they persevered and pursued their dreams and opportunities. Their legacy lives on through their descendants.

It is true that our lives are much easier in many ways than those of our ancestors, and we owe a great deal to the struggles and sacrifices of the generations that came before us. Our ancestors faced challenges that we can only imagine, and it is important to remember and honour them.

Spiritualism has a significant place in Scottish culture, and many believe that the spirits of our ancestors still exist around us. Lighting a candle or talking about them is a way to honour their memory and to keep them close. In a way—to keep them alive.

Our family both recent and past have played an important role in shaping who we are today. By remembering them, we can carry on their legacy and continue to draw strength from their struggles and accomplishments. They are who we are.

People must know the past to understand the present and to face the future.

—Nellie McClung

A Collaborative Effort

Thanks to the preservation of records, advancements in technology, and the widespread use of DNA analysis, we have the remarkable ability to journey back in time to learn about the lives of our ancestors and the events that helped shape their lives. I am grateful to all the people who have helped me discover my ancestors' stories.

Several years after Sarah Isabella Brown Rains (1911–1993) had helped me to get started on my research on my maternal Brown relatives, I had the opportunity and privilege to correspond with James "Garfield" Buchanan, the grandson of Mary Brown Fisher (1851–1939) and my second cousin once removed. He had been working on his Fisher family tree for many years and had travelled to Scotland as part of his research. Garfield provided me with copies of documents pertaining to the Brown and Granger family that he had retrieved from the archives in Edinburgh. I will be forever grateful that he shared them with me.

Years later, when I completed my DNA, a door was flung wide open for me; it allowed me to find ancestors and descendants in Scotland, England, Australia, and closer to home in Canada and the United States.

Some of the distant relatives that I encountered were also very interested in documenting and preserving their own family histories, and we were able to collaborate and encourage each other as we searched for our elusive ancestors.

Family lore had always been that the Browns were from Strathaven, south of Glasgow, but as we pooled our findings, we learned that although some had certainly lived near there, that is not where the Browns had originated from. It was not until I had connected with these distant relatives that I finally discovered that the Browns had come from the west coast of Scotland, and from the Isles of Luing and Islay and Easdale Island of the Inner Hebrides.

As often happens in small geographical areas, intermarriages were common, and in this case, marriages of the Browns with the McDonalds, the Campbells, the McKays, and another Brown family made it difficult to sort them all out. However, with the help of my DNA cousins—Gary Rains, Sonja Devereux Broad, Neil Brown, Allan MacDougall, and Eric Hutton—we have now been able to piece together the lives of some of our ancestors and thus determine how we are all connected.

In addition to my long-lost cousins, I would like to acknowledge Iain McDougall, director of the Easdale Island Folk Museum, and Tim Sinclair, from the Slate Islands Archives, for their generous assistance and photographs; these were of great help in telling my story.

As family storytellers, we spend our days uncovering the rich, complex stories of those who came before us. There are, however, many mysteries that still remain.

I hope that a descendant from this branch of the Brown family will take up the mantle of this project and continue the quest, thereby unearthing at least some of the many missing pieces of the story. I also encourage them to document the stories of new generations that emerge; in this way, future descendants will be able to gain both an insight into and an appreciation of the lives of even more of their ancestors who blazed the trail.

Through this important work, we, as our ancestors' heirs, will continue the task of preserving our family's legacy and of honouring the many sacrifices of those who came before us.

Part VIII

Reflections on Family

Beachdan mu Theaghlach

Rodger Brown (1877–1957).

Born in Glasgow. The great-grandson of Dugald Brown (1783–1862) and Mary McCallum (1783–1866). Rodger was at one time a steelworker who walked about fourteen kilometers to work each day and then the same distance home again.

Agnes Josephine Brown (1890–1940).

Born in Roma, Queensland, Australia. The daughter of Duncan Brown (1854–1918) and Agnes Glenn (1861–1914). The granddaughter of Alexander Brown (1827–1868) and Catherine McQueen (1829–1908). Agnes was an opera star in Sydney; she used the stage name Anita Roma.

Christina McCulloch Brown (1897–1964).

Born in Glasgow. The daughter of Peter Brown (1858–1923) and Mary Rogers (1867–1940). The granddaughter of Alexander Brown (1827–1868) and Catherine McQueen (1829–1908).

Allan, Susan, and Jessica Henderson.

Born in Brisbane, Australia. The great-grandchildren of Duncan Henderson (1821–1895) and Janet Brown (1821–1855).

Allan MacDougall (1885-1968).

Born in Kilbrandon, Argyll, Scotland. Son of Alexander MacDougall (1852–1926) and Margaret Brown (1856–1942). Nephew to John Brown Sr. (1818-1901) of St. Joseph Island. Allan worked as a slate quarrier on Easdale Island. He served with distinction in the 5th Battalion Highland Light Infantry during the First World War and was awarded the Distinguished Conduct Medal for his actions.

Hugh Brown (1877-1959), Donald Brown (1874-1944)
and Dugald Brown (1872-1927).

Born in Glasgow. The great-grandsons of Dugald Brown (1783-1862) and Mary McCallum (1783–1866). Hugh emigrated to the United States in about 1912 and then to Canada. He lived in the Niagara Falls area.

Hugh Brown (1877-1959), wife Christina McLachlan,and
sons John McCulloch Brown and Andrew McLachlan Brown.

Hugh Brown was the great-grandson of Dugald Brown (1783-
1862) and Mary McCallum (1783–1866).

Marjorie Maye Harmon (1928-1999).

Born in Detroit. The great-granddaughter of John McLarty (1847-1919) and Janet Brown (1845-1876).

DNA cousins meet in Scotland. 2024. (left to right) Sonja Broad Devereux (England), Allan MacDougall (Scotland), and Eric Hutton (Canada).

All descendants of Alexander Brown (1754-?) and Christian McDonald (1756-?).

Appendix A
Generations

1. Alexander Brown and Christian McDonald

   Children:

   Dugald Brown (1783–1862) married Mary McCallum (1783–1866).
   Janet Brown (1784–?).
   Duncan Brown (1789–1874) married Janet McDonald (1790–1855).
   Catherine Brown (1791–?)
   Donald Brown (1792–1865) married Mary McCowan (1795–1878).
   John Brown (1792–?).
   Hugh Brown (1795–1869) married Ann McDonald (1798–1841).

2. Dugald Brown and Mary McCallum

   Children:

   Janet Brown (1804–1885) married John McKay (1803–1879)
   Mary Brown (1807–?)
   Hugh Brown (1813–1885) married Janet McCulloch (1815–1881)
   Dugald Brown (1814–?) married Catherine McDougall (1817–?)
   Ann/Agnes Brown (1826–1877) married John Brown (1823–1901)

3. Duncan Brown and Janet McDonald

   Children:

   John Brown (1818–1901) married Janet Granger (1821–?)
   Janet/Jean Brown (1821–1855) married Duncan Henderson (1821–1895)
   Donald Brown (1823–1887) married Margaret McDonald (1830–1903)
   Mary Brown (1825–1901) married John Harroway (1826–1891)
   Alexander Brown (1827–1868) married Catherine McQueen (1829–1908)
   Duncan Brown (1830–?)
   Sarah/Sally Brown (1832–1896) married Donald McKay (1828–1872)
   Ann Brown (1834–?)

4. Donald Brown and Mary McCowan

Children:

John Brown (1815–1898) married Mary Brown (1813–1894)
Alexander Brown (1819–1900) married Elizabeth McQueen (1825–1911)
Mary Brown (1825–1896) married Donald McMillan (1821–1899)
Donald Brown (1825–1887) married Sarah Ferguson (1830–1905)
Christina Brown (1827–1909)
Ann Brown (1831–1888) married Neil Baxter (1826–1873)
James Brown (1834–1865)
Norman Brown (1836–1873) married Barbara McFarlane (1840–1896)
Catherine Brown (1843–1914) married John Johnston (1843–1914)

5. John Brown

No marriage or children

6. Hugh Brown and Ann McDonald

Children:

Alexander Brown (1816–1859) married Catherine McLean (1818–?)
Mary Brown (1821–1900)
John Brown (1826–1861) married Ann McKay (1837–1910)
Christine Brown (1827–1903)
Dugald Brown (1829–1909)
Gilbert Brown (1831-?)

7. John Brown and Janet Granger

Children:

Marion Brown (1843–1930) married John Henry (1833–1915)
Janet/Jessie Brown (1845–1876) married John McLarty (1847–1919)
Helen Brown (1848–1853)
Mary Brown (1851–1939) married Richard Fisher (1833–1903)
Helen/Ellen Brown (1854–1943) married Thomas Welsh (1852–1917)
Sarah Brown (1857–1936) married John Kirk (1836–1915)
John Brown (1859–1932) married Prudence Shipman (1864–1949)
Alexander "Sandy" Brown (1862–1937) married Isabella Wood (1876–1966)

8. Janet Brown and Duncan Henderson

Children:

Duncan Henderson (1843–1920) married Isabella Fairlie (1852–1922)
Donald Henderson (1845–1910) married Mary McFarlane (1848–?)
Catherine Henderson (1847–1928) married James Kerr (1845–?)
Janet Henderson (1850–1855)
Mary Henderson (1854–1855)

9. Donald Brown and Margaret McDonald

Children:

Catherine Brown (1850–?)
Jessie Brown (1852–1907) married Hugh McKillop (1851–1918)
Margaret Brown (1854–1942) married Alexander McDougall (1852–1926)
Duncan Brown (1855–1891)
John Brown (1858–1927)
Ann Brown (1860–1905) married Hugh Campbell (1857–1930)
Sarah Brown (1862–1937) married William Laird (1863–1922)
Colin Brown (1865–1946) married Jessie McKay (1870–1916)
Isabella Brown (1868–1951) married William Johnston (1869–1937)
Jane Brown (1870–1872)

10. Mary Brown and John Harroway

Children:

Christina Harroway (adopted) (1857–1940) married John Sanderson (1856–1913)
John Harroway (1859–1919) married Annie Stewart (1873–1933)
William Harroway (1861–1868)

11. Alexander Brown and Catherine McQueen

Children:

Duncan Brown (1854–1918) married Agnes Glenn (1861–1914)
John Brown (1856–1924) married Mary Millar (1859–1933)
Peter Brown (1858–1923) married Mary Rogers (1867–1940)
Alexander Brown (1863–1915) married Jeanie Ferguson (1867–1943)
Catherine Brown (1867–1924) married William Main (1849–1915)

12. Duncan Brown (1830–?)

13. Sarah Brown and Donald McKay

Children:

John McKay (1864–1907)
Ann McKay (1866–1919) married Hugh Smith (1867–1918)
Jessie McKay (1866–1879)
Archibald McKay (1868–1874)
Donald McKay (1870–1938) married Susan Harkins (1878–1931)

14. Ann Brown (1834–?)

15. Marion Brown and John Henry

Children:

William Henry (1869–1946) married Susan Evans (1878–1941)
Simon Henry (1871–1931) married Laura Davis (1876–1944)
John Henry (1873–1952) married Emma Johnston (1880–1941)
George Henry (1876–1960) married Theresa Davis (1874–1965)
James Henry (1877–1950) married Annie Patterson (1876–1945)
Albert Henry (1879–1954) married Gladys Pickard (1885–1972)
Jessie Henry (1883–1966) married Donald Cameron (1875–1944)
Marion Henry (1886–1964) married Frederick Burgess (1890–1970)

16. Janet/Jessie Brown and John McLarty

Children:

Agnes "Mary" McLarty (1874–1948) married William Harmon (1866–1945)

17. Helen Brown (1848–1853)

18. Mary Brown and Richard Fisher

Children:

Janet Fisher (1880–1974) married William McGregor (1880–1958)
Richard Fisher (1881–1958)
Catherine Fisher (1883–1974) married Benjamin Archibald (1878–1959)
George Fisher (1885–1959)
Sarah Fisher (1889–1974) married James Buchanan (1885–1967)

19. Helen/Ellen Brown and Thomas Welsh

Children:

Fredrick Welsh (1876–1964) married Hazel Bennet (1889–1946)
Thomas Welsh (1879–1900)
Bessie Welsh (1881–1937) married Wilson Shingle (1877–1952)
Katherine Welsh (1883–1956) married Edward Busby (1879–1955)
William Welsh (1885–1972) married Laura Miller (1888–1920)
Annie Welsh (1888–1953) married George Brunton (1889–1951)
Edward Welsh (1891–1951) married Irene McPhee (1891–1974)
Mary Welsh (1894–1979) married Earl Madill (1891–1955)

20. Sarah Brown and John Kirk

Children:

Joseph Kirk (1881–1958) married Maria McFadden (1895–1977)
John Kirk (1883–1928) married Marie Krause (1891–1947)
George Kirk (1886–1886)
Richard Kirk (1890–1927)

21. John Brown and Prudence Shipman

Children:

John Brown (1882–1926) married Lillian Sanderson (1875–1960)
Jessie Brown (1885–1954) married Arken Eddy (1883–1961)
Margaret Brown (1888–1944) married Fay Eddy (1884–1950)
Olive Brown (1897–1897)
Lawrence Brown (1906–1957) married Helen Hyland (1916–1986)

22. Alexander "Sandy" Brown and Isabella Wood

Children:

John Duncan "Dunc" Brown (1898–1975) married Blanche Cooper (1897–1947)
Mary Brown (1900–1955) married William Snider (1902–1976)
Hazel Brown (1903–1939) married Bernie Gay (1898–1977)
Gladys Brown (1905–1988) married Ernest Snider (1905–1976)
Launcelot Brown (1908–1929)
Sarah Brown (1911–1993) married Glynn Rains (1909–1958)
Emily Brown (1914–1915)
William Brown (1915–1915)

23. John Brown and Blanche Cooper

Children:

Lloyd Brown (1926–1975) married Catherine Cain (1932–1989)
Harold Brown (1930–2013) married Coyla Anderson (1931–2014)
Marguerite Brown (1931–1932)
Emily "Betty" Brown (1934–2004) married Wilfred "Bill" Haight (1931–2004)

The End
An Deireadh

Heilan Coo. Bò Ghàidhealach.[88]

Endnotes

1. House of Names. Brown Family Crest. Accessed April 6, 2025
    https://www.houseofnames.com/ca/brown-family-crest/scottish

2. Riley, M.E. The Scottish Wifey. 2003 Accessed March 28, 2025.
    http://www.marariley.net/celtic/scotland.htm

3. Brawley, Anthony. "Forgotten History - Scotland's Slate Islands," Eclectica
    (blog), July, 2011, https://addiator.blogspot.com/2011/07 /forgotten-history-
    scotlands-slate.html. With permission.

4. "Slate Islands and Scarba Map," Southern Hebrides of Scotland, Southern
    Hebrides, accessed January 23,2024, https://www.southernhebrides.com/
    slate-islands-and-scarba-map/ Image reproduced with permission.

5. "The Inner Hebrides and Outer Hebrides," Wikipedia, Wikimedia Foundation,
    Kelisi, last modified August 4, 2007, 09:19, https://en.wikipedia.org/wiki/
    Hebrides#/media/File:Hebridesmap.png.

6. "Hogmanay Celebration" AI generated (Microsoft Copilot). March 2024.

7. "Master Shoemaker and Apprentices." AI generated (Dall-E). February 2024.

8. "Slate Islands and Scarba Map" Southern Hebrides of Scotland, Southern
    Hebrides published January 23, 2025 https://www.southernhebrides.com/
    slate-islands-and-scarba-map/. Image reproduced with permission

9. "Photographs – Page 2," Slate Islands Archives, The Scottish Slate Islands
    Heritage Trust, accessed January 23, 2025, https:// sites.google.com/view/
    slateislandsarchives/photos/photos-2. Image reproduced with permission
    from Slate Islands Archives

10. "Winning the Slate," Slate Islands Heritage Trust, Slate Island Heritage Trust
    2018 – 2024, accessed January 17, 2024, https://slateislands.org.uk/winning-
    the-slate/. Image reproduced with permission from Slate Islands Archives
    in January 2024.

11. "Cottages Easdale Island" Photo Credit Walter Baxter https://argyllcoast.
    co.uk/islands-of-argyll/easdale.html Image reproduced with permission
    Walter Baxter

12. "Archives E-M Easdale 1," Slate Island Archives, The Scottish Slate Islands Heritage Trust, accessed January 23, 2024, https://sites.google.com/view/slateislandsarchives/museumarchives/e-m. Image reproduced with permission from Slate Islands Archives in January 2024.

13. "Social History," Easdale Island Folk Museum, Easdale Island Folk Museum, last modified January 17, 2025, https://www.easdalemuseum.org/social-history/. Image reproduced with permission from Easdale Island Folk Museum

14. Photo Credit Allan MacDougall.

15. Photo Credit Neil Brown.

16. "Creag Nam Duin or Hill Quarry" accessed January 24, 2025. https://www.easdalemuseum.org/slate-industry/ Image reproduced with permission Easdale Folk Museum

17. The Hellish Rabble Easdale Folk Museum. Accessed December 13, 2024 https://www.easdalemuseum.org/slate-industry/ Image reproduced with permission Easdale Folk Museum

18. "Eilean Eisdeal: Newsletter Archive," Eilean Eisdeal, Eilean Eisdeal, last modified December 25, 2024, https://www.easdale.org/news/index.htm. Image reproduced with permission from Eilean Eisdeal Archive in December 2024.

19. "Easdale Island harbour" Slate Island Archives accessed January 23, 2024. https://sites.google.com/view/slateislandsarchives/photos/photos-2 Image reproduced with permission Slate Island Archives

20. "From Island of Seil". Slate Island Archives. Accessed January 13, 2024. https://sites.google.com/view/slateislandsarchives/photos/photos-3 Image reproduced with permission Slate Island Archives

21. "Easdale Quarry Men".Slate Island Archives. Accessed January 23, 2024. https://sites.google.com/view/slateislandsarchives/photos/photos-3 Image reproduced with permission Slate Island Archives .

22. "PHOTOGRAPHS - Page 3," Slate Islands Archives, The Scottish Slate Islands Heritage Trust, accessed January 24, 2025, https://sites.google.com/view/slateislands archives/photos/photos-3. Image reproduced with permission from Slate Islands Archives in January 2024.

23. "Kingston, 1911," Glasgow Life Virtual Mitchell, Mitchell Library, accessed January 24, 2025, https://www.mitchelllibrary.org/virtualmitchell/

view-item?key=VXsiUCI6eyJOYXgiOjEsInQiOls1NV19fQ&pg=7&WINID
=1733678943263#8XVEuluq0uoAAAGTp1ebWw/6468. Mitchell Library
public domain.

24. "Annan, Thomas – Nahaufnahme, Nr. 115 High Street (Zeno Fotografie),"
    Picryl, Get Archive LLC, accessed January 23, 2025, https://picryl.com/
    media/annan-thomas-nahaufnahme-nr-115-high-street-zeno-fotografie-
    d7e445. Public domain.

25. Annan, Thomas "Glasgow Tenements - The Old Closes and Streets of
    Glasgow". "University of Glasgow Library." Accessed January 23, 2025
    https://universityofglasgowlibrary.wordpress.com/2020/08/13/asc-
    rewind-the-old-closes-and-streets-of-glasgow/ Public domain.

26. Lanarkshire is no longer a county. It is now part of the council area
    of North Lanarkshire and South Lanarkshire.

27. AI generated (Dall-E). February 2024.

28. "Child labour in Glasgow factories," Amalgamate, Amalgamate Safety Risk
    Management Ltd, last modified May 16, 2024, http://www.amalgamate-
    safety.com/wp-content/uploads/2018/06/ChildLabour.png. Public domain.

29. "Govan St/Muirhead St," Glasgow Life Virtual Mitchell, Mitchell Library,
    accessed January 23, 2025, https://www.mitchelllibrary.org/virtualmitchell/
    view-item?key=VXsiUCI6eyJOYXgiOjEsInQiOls1XX19&pg=166&WIN-
    ID=1733678943263#8XVEuluq0uoAAAGTp1ebWw/5762. Mitchell Library
    public domain.

30. "Flying Cloud (clipper)," Wikipedia, Wikimedia Foundation, last
    modified March 10, 2025, https://en.wikipedia.org/wiki/Flying_
    Cloud_%28clipper%29. Public domain image.

31. "Emigration and emigrants," The National Archives of the UK, His Majesty's
    Government, last modified January 20, 2025, https://www.nationalarchives.
    gov.uk/help-with-your-research/research-guides/emigration/#7-emigration-
    to-australia. Public domain.

32. AI generated (Dall-E). November 2023.

33. "Regents Canal 1950". Accessed March 14, 2024. https://www.angelboat.org/
    archive#bwg2/37 Public Domain

34. "Distilled Sunshine" Brewing beer. Access February 3, 2024
    https://distilledsunshine.wordpress.com/2020/04/04/why-did-
    farmers-first-make-beer-wine-and-whisky/ Public Domain

35. "Duke St/High St, 1897," Glasgow Life Virtual Mitchell, Mitchell Library, accessed January 3, 2025, https://www.mitchelllibrary.org/virtualmitchell / view-item?key=VXsiUCI6eyJ0YXgiOjEsInQiOls0NTJdfX0&pg=51&WINID =1733678943263#8XVEuluq0uoAAAGTp1ebWw/5024. Mitchell Library public domain.

36. Glasgow City Archives Photograph by Robt. Houston. Family Butcher Mitchell Library retrieved September 17, 2025, https://theglasgowstory. com/image/?inum=TGSE00870.

37. "Argyll and Bute Hospital," Wikipedia, Wikimedia Foundation, Steven Brown, published February 22, 2025, https://commons.wikimedia.org/wiki/ File:Argyll_and_Bute_Hospital _(geograph _1684498).jpg.

38. "30 Ardgowan Pl," Glasgow Life Virtual Mitchell, Mitchell Library, accessed January 13, 2025, https://www.mitchelllibrary.org/virtualmitchell/ view-item?key=VXsiUCI6eyJ0YXgiOjEsInQiOlsxNTRdfX0&WINID= 1733678943263&fullPage=1#8XVEuluq0uoAAAGTp1ebWw/1780. Mitchell Library public domain.

39. AI generated (Microsoft Copilot). February 2024.

40. "76 Crown St." Glasgow Life Virtual Mitchell, Mitchell Library accessed January 23, 2025 Public domain. https://www.mitchelllibrary.org/virtual-mitchell/search-results?key=VXsiUCI6eyJ0YXgiOjEsInQiOls1XX19&WIN-ID=1743013574458&pg=

41. Glasgow City Archives Ref P663. Accessed January 23, 2025. https://www.researchgate.net/figure/GCA-P1891-Glasgow-Juvenile-Delinquency-Board-Glasgow-1886_fig1_382324013 Public Domain

42. Michael Allsion "Welcome to the Glasgow City Poorhouse," Old Glasgow (blog), December 18, 2014, https://oldglasgow.tumblr.com/post /105544160131/welcome-to-the-glasgow-city-poorhouse-originally.

43. "Queen's Dock," Glasgow Life Virtual Mitchell, Mitchell Library, accessed January 23, 2025, https://www.mitchelllibrary.org/virtualmitchell/ view-item?i=7506&WINID=1742158436035. Mitchell Library public domain.

44. Photo Credit M. Galbraith.

45. AI generated (Microsoft Copilot). December 2024.

46. Photo Credit Robert Currie Collection.

47. Photo Credit Robert Currie Collection.

48. "Burnhead Farm," Geograph, Richard Sutcliffe, published January 7, 2019, https://www.geograph.org.uk/photo/5812053.

49. AI generated (Dall-E). February 2024.

50. Sept 17, 1848 Brown, Helen (Old Parish Registers Birth 621/40 175 Avondale) National Records of Scotland

51. Annie Ellen Brown and Thomas Welsh. December 30, 1878. Marriage registration, Marriage Records, 1867–1952. Port Huron, Michigan, U.S.

52. AI generated (Dall-E). November 2023.

53. "Emigration to the Province of Ontario, 1869," Archives of Ontario, Ministry of Public and Business Service Delivery, Ontario, last modified July 5, 2024, http://www.archives.gov.on.ca/en/explore/online/agriculture/big/big_22_emigration_poster.aspx.

54. Brett Lockwood, "They're Giving Away Land!," O' Canada (blog), April 11, 2015, https://ocanadablog.com/2015/04/11/theyre-giving-away-land/#jp-carousel-4589.

55. AI generated (Microsoft Copilot). February 2024.

56. "The Allan Line," Norway-Heritage, Børge Solem, last modified January 14, 2025, http://www.norwayheritage.com/p_shiplist.asp?co=allan.

57. Waldensian Off Greenock ."The Allan Line Clyde River and Firth Ships Firth Ships and Steamers." Accessed March 11, 2024. https://www.dalmadan.com/?p=1044

58. P. C. Kohler, "Allan Line Apex: R.M.S. Alsatian & Calgarian," Wanted on Voyage (blog), February 16, 2021, https://wantedonthevoyage.blogspot.com/2021/02/.

59. AI generated (OpenArt). February 2025.

60. AI generated (Microsoft Co-Pilot). August 2024.

61. "Quarantine Station Building," Specialized Media Section Slide Library - Photo Reference Catalogue [graphic material], D.A. McLaughlin/Library and Archives Canada, accessed March 17, 2025, https://recherche-collection-search.bac-lac.gc.ca/eng/home/Record?idnumber=3192439&app=FonAndCol&ecopy=c079029.

62. "Full record for Brown, John," The Canadian County Atlas Digital Project, McGill University, accessed November 13, 2024, https://digital.library.mcgill.ca/countyatlas/showrecord.php?PersonID=103458.

63. "Full record for Henry, John," The Canadian County Atlas Digital Project, Rare Books and Special Collections McGill University Libraries, accessed January 23, 2025, https://digital.library.mcgill.ca/countyatlas/showrecord.php?PersonID=103691.

64. "Marion Brown Henry," Memorials, Find a Grave, August 21, 2020, https://www.findagrave.com/memorial/184424234/marion-henry/sitmap_index.xml#view-photo=211270313.

65. "Great Western Railway of Canada," Toronto Railway Historical Association, Toronto Railway Historical Association, last modified November 30, 2024, https://www.trha.ca/trha/history/railways/great-western-railway-of-canada/. Public domain.

66. "The Reverend Robert Hall (0490ph)," Picture St. Marys, Public Libarary and the St. Marys Museum, accessed January 24 , 2025 https://images.ourontario.ca/stmarys/45829/data. Public domain.

67. "Janet McLarty," Memorials, Find a Grave, accessed January 2025, https://www.findagrave.com/memorial/221434727/janet-mclarty/sitemap_index.xml#view-photo=275797551.

68. Photo Credit W. Bryant.

69. Grand Trunk Railway Station St. Marys Ontario Accessed December 16, 2024 https://images.ourontario.ca/stmarys/details.asp?ID=48362 Public domain.

70. "Excursion season, 1878, Northern Railway of Canada and Great Rail and Lake Connections," QSpace: Queen's Scholarship & Digital Collections, Queen's University, accessed April 17, 2024, https://qspace.library .queensu.ca/server/api/core/bitstreams/c7e2df98-aed1-49dc-9051-fed387788372/content.

71. "Northern Belle (1875 ship)," Wikipedia, Wikimedia Foundation, last modified September 27, 2023, https://en.wikipedia.org/wiki/Northern Belle_(1875_ship).

72. "Northern Advance, June 20, 1878 edition," Our Ontario, owner or sponsor of the site, accessed April 13, 2024, https://images.ourontario .ca/Partners/Barrie/na/BaPL002763656pf_0320.pdf.

73. "Northern Railway of Canada and Great Rail & Lake Connections," Wikipedia, Wikimedia Foundation, accessed June 14, 2024, https://upload.wikimedia.org/wikipedia/commons/e/e9/Northern_railway_of _Canada_and_Great_rail_%26_lake_connections_%28IA_northernrail wayo00nort%29.pdf.

74. Post card collection Lee Ann Holmes Miller.

75. Photo Credit C R. Thompson.

76. "Agriculture in Algoma Rural Agri-Innovation Network" accessed March 28, 2025 https://rainalgoma.ca/rain-agriculture/algoma/

77. "The London Asylum for the Insane", Ivey Family London Room, accessed December 14, 2024 https://www.lib.uwo.ca/archives/virtualexhibits/londonasylum/

78. "How Immigrants and Others Were Enticed to Build Farms from the Forests,"The Observer (Sarnia), Postmedia Network, published November 24, 2015, Public Domain https://www.theobserver.ca/2015/11/23/how-immigrants-and-others-were-enticed-to-build-farms-from-the-forests#:~:text=Ontario %20enticed%20them%20to%20head,for%2050%20cents%20an%20acre.

79. "Olive Brown," Memorials, Find a Grave, accessed January 16, 2025, https://www.findagrave.com/memorial/133938068/olive-brown#view-photo=109389513.

80. AI generated (Microsoft Copilot). August 2024.

81. "Smallpox," Museum of Healthcare at Kingston, Last modified September 19, 2024, https://www.museumofhealthcare.ca/explore/exhibits/vaccinations/smallpox.html

82. "Library of Congress. Farm Security Administration - Office of War Information Photograph Collection." "Person Collecting Sap from a Tree in Snowy Landscape (Reproduction number: LC-USF33-011158-M4). https://www.loc.gov/pictures/collection/fsa/

83. "Harvest Train Arriving in Western Canada." Private collection of Our Miramichi Family (1940).

84. "Popular Searches of the Local History Collections Database," Saskatoon Public Library, Local History Room, Saskatoon Public Library,. published August 17, 2016, http://spldatabase.saskatoonlibrary.ca/ics-wpd/exec/icswppro.dll?AC=QBE_QUERY&TN=LHR_RAD&N-P=4&QB0=AND&QF0=CLASSIFICATION&QI0=HARVEST-ING*&QB1=AND&QF1=DECADES&QI1=1920S&MR=20&RF=www_Canned%20Searches&QB2=AND&QF2=THUMBNAIL_IMAGE&QI2=*.

85. AI generated (Microsoft Copilot). December 2024.

86. "Great Lakes Vessel History Royalton 1" accessed February 24, 2025
     https://www.greatlakesvesselhistory.com/histories-by-name/r/royalton-1
     Public domain.

87. "Loading hay into barn, 1919," Archives of Ontario, Ministry of Public
     and Business Service Delivery, Ontario, last modified October 9, 2024,
     https://www.archives.gov.on.ca/en/explore/online/agriculture/big/big_56_
     loading_hay.aspx. Public domain.

88. AI generated (Microsoft Copilot). March 2024.

www.ingramcontent.com/pod-product-compliance
Lightning Source LLC
Chambersburg PA
CBHW051300120626
46547CB00015B/2028